How Long Can a Fly Fly?

HOW LONG CAN A FLY FLY?

175 ANSWERS TO POSSIBLE AND IMPOSSIBLE QUESTIONS ABOUT ANIMALS

LARS-ÅKE JANZON

SELECTION AND EDITING:
SUSANNE LILJENSTRÖM

TRANSLATED BY LISA LINDBERG

SKYHORSE PUBLISHING

Publisher's note: *How Long Can a Fly Fly?* was originally published in Sweden, so readers may notice the book contains a large number of facts about animals in Scandinavia, in addition to trivia about animals around the world.

Visit our website at www.skyhorsepublishing.com.

10 9 8 7 6 5 4 3 2 1

Library of Congress Cataloging-in-Publication Data is available on file.

ISBN: 978-1-62087-065-5

Printed in China

CONTENTS

ON DUTY BIOLOGIST WITH ALL THE ANSWERS!

When Lars-Åke Janzon turns on his cellphone in his home in Stockholm, it sometimes happens that the phone starts ringing at six o'clock in the morning. Like when the dreaded Black Widow spider was found a few years ago in a garage a little north of the city. At times like that he is flooded with calls from radio and newspapers, and invited to every morning news talk show on TV.

Lars-Åke Janzon is an On Duty Biologist at the Museum of Natural History in Sweden, and is constantly prepared to answer everyone's questions about animals and nature. If duty calls he will not hesitate to participate in a live radio show from his cellphone on the bus going to work. Luckily Lars-Åke is not someone who is easily stressed. He is a cheerful and friendly person with a twinkle in his eye and is everyone's favorite on both radio and television.

The On Duty Biologist has an office in the southern wing of the museum. As soon as you enter the room you understand that a constant quest for answers to nature's mysteries is taking place: The high walls are covered by bursting bookshelves with titles like *The World of Fossils*,

Animal Records, Sharks and Rays, Die Wildbienen, Animals' Poison, and Carl von Linnés *Swedish Flora.*

On the table amidst stacks of *The Entomological Journal, The Swedish Botanical Journal,* and *Our World of Birds,* you find plastic bags with parts of green plants—sent by someone who wanted to know what sort of exotic plant was growing in the backyard—and a see-through plastic box with beechnuts, oak, a number of real chestnuts, and other things for a curious biologist. A few red and slightly frail geraniums are shining in the window, and on the table in front of them stands a stereo microscope.

"I used it just the other day, to study a little insect that someone found in their bathroom and wanted to know if it was a pest. I only had a few parts, like some of the head and the middle of the body, but I could still see that it was a small Heteroptera, nothing to worry about!" Janzon announced energetically.

So what is the best part of being an On Duty Biologist?
"The diversity," Lars-Åke answers instantly. "Diversity in regard to the questions I receive but also the diversity of people I meet in emails and on the phone. Most of all the children, from preschool age to middle school, not yet stifled by school and therefore still thinking in ways that could be considered as strange. All the *difficult* questions are asked by children!

"For example, 'How big is the mouth of a worm?' and 'How long is the tongue of a worm?'

Luckily I have a colleague who is an expert at worms . . . "

What few people know is that the Museum of Natural History in Stockholm not only holds exhibitions and stuffed animals, it is also a big research institution. Of the roughly

250 employees, almost 200 conduct research, including the collections and administration departments. That is why Lars-Åke, as a newly graduated biologist in the fall of 1972, started out taking care of the insect collection in the entomological section. Then a few years of moving around the different departments in the museum followed; he boiled seal skulls for the collections of skeletons, made pollen forecasts, was the editor of the journal *Fauna and Flora*, and produced exhibitions before he returned to focus on entomology to receive a PhD degree. In 1984 he defended a thesis about Hymenoptera, who live off of maggots in potted flowers.

"But after a while it started feeling somewhat introverted; we were the only three people in the world that were experts on the species in a relatively small group within the big Hymenoptera parasitic genus *Pteromalus*."

That is why he did not hesitate when he was offered the job as an On Duty Biologist almost ten years ago. Throughout the years he has answered more than 100,000 questions from the public, not including the ones from radio, television, and newspapers.

Suddenly Lars-Åke's cellphone beeps: GREAT EGRET IN HASSLEHOLM the display reads. Lars-Åke is an ornithologist and a member of Club 300, for those who enjoy seeing many and rare bird species. The club has an alarm system so that the members can quickly communicate with each other when a rare bird is spotted somewhere in the country.

Lars-Åke does not want to call himself a professional, and does not know exactly how many species of birds he has really seen. A little reluctantly, he admits that the number is probably close to 350. Although he rarely heads to the site

11

himself, when the alarm goes off, it can be helpful for him to be aware of the sighting.

"All of a sudden someone calls and ask about some strange bird they have seen. Then I ask where they live and if it is nearby Hässleholm—bingo!"

The questions of the "What was it that I saw?" variety are becoming increasingly common in the On Duty Biologist's box of questions. As more and more people have access to a digital camera it is easier to take a photo to send in whenever you see something interesting, from a hairy larva, a new butterfly, or an unusual spider.

"And it is a lot of fun! It is just those things we are good at here in the museum, our specialty is knowledge about species, kinship, and evolution."

Lars-Åke Janzon was born in Malmö, Sweden, but grew up in a Stockholm suburb. He became a field biologist early on, and the fascination with birds, insects, and plants has not lessened throughout the years. He admits that his passion for nature can be a burden for people around him when taking walks together; there is always something new to discover and study. To categorize even the most common bird can be a challenge, as its appearance varies depending on age, gender, time of year, and mating costume.

As an On Duty Biologist, Lars-Åke has become one of the most well-known faces in the Museum of Natural History. Sometimes he feels like an actual celebrity. Such as when a young kid on his bicycle stops and asks him: "Are you the person in Hjärnkontoret?" And with a voice full of admiration exclaims: "You have the answers to everything—you are awesome!"

Susanne Liljenström

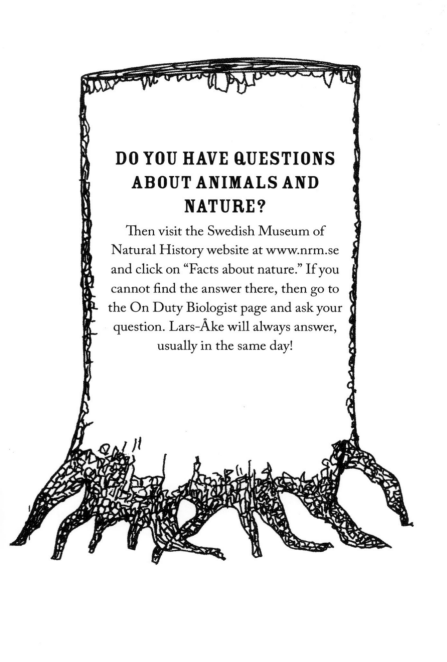

DO YOU HAVE QUESTIONS ABOUT ANIMALS AND NATURE?

Then visit the Swedish Museum of Natural History website at www.nrm.se and click on "Facts about nature." If you cannot find the answer there, then go to the On Duty Biologist page and ask your question. Lars-Åke will always answer, usually in the same day!

WHAT
ANIMALS
DO

SWIM, FLY, JUMP, AND RUN

Can fish swim backwards?

Yes, there are several fish species that can swim backward. But most of them are really only drifting with the current.

Butterflyfish belong to the group of fish that actually swim backwards on purpose. It is a group of fish with flat, thin bodies, usually with a line next to the eye and sometimes a dark spot near the tail fin. The pattern works as a camouflage or defense mechanism that confuses predatory fish so that they bite at the wrong end of the prey.

Another fish that can swim backward is the tanganyika-cichlid *Triglachromis otostigma*. It lives in the muddy ground regions of the Tanganyika Lake between Tanzania and Congo and it has developed bendable fin tips on its pectoral fins. By swimming backward, the fish can use its pectoral

fins to dig up insect larvae that are hidden in the mud. The Knifefish, or "Black Ghost," *Apteronotus albifrons*, can swim both forward and backward, and even upside down!

❋{ MYTH }❋

Crayfish also swim backward when they are frightened. That they crawl backward, on the other hand, is a myth. We should therefore not say that crayfish can walk backward!

Can bumblebees fly?

That bumblebees cannot fly is an old student myth. According to the myth, bumblebees are too heavy, too round, and equipped with wings far too small to fly. This is of course not true; bumblebees are in fact well equipped to fly.

The rumor of the bumblebee's inability to fly has its own story. It probably originates from a student joke at the Institute of Technology in Stockholm. The mathematical measurements that were published in the student newspaper *Brux* were made without considering the bumblebee's wing movements. The truth is that bumblebees cannot glide, an characteristic they share with most other insects.

If you remove the thick fur coat, the bumblebee body is quite similar to the regular Western Honey Bee. In some regards the bumblebee's ability to fly can even outperform regular bees; for example, they can fly in winds up to about 9 mph, while honey bees face a problem at only 4 mph.

That bumblebees cannot hear is, on the other hand, completely true, but they do have an excellent sense of smell.

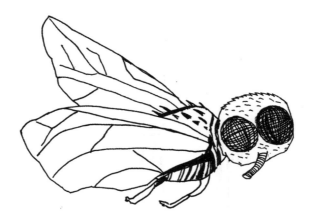

How long can a fly fly?

Generally speaking, insects are sensitive to wind and they try to find more calm places when it is windy. But of course there are differences between different species—there are about 4,500 different kinds of flies in Sweden.

Some horse flies can get up to 1.18 inches long and relatively heavy; they handle wind better than a housefly. But how many miles per hour can they go? That research still remains to be done! However, the On Duty Biologist has done some observations on his own: One summer day when he started his car the side windows were full of flies, probably houseflies. Most of them disappeared quite fast when the car accelerated, but not all of them. The fly that held on the longest was sitting on the left side of the car window and did not give up until the speedometer showed over 43 mph.

BY THE WAY...

In only one second a cockroach can run its own body length times thirty. It usually only runs very short distances, for example to escape the light from a lamp turned on in darkness. But when it runs, it runs fast!

TOP SPEED FOR A FEW COMMON NORDIC ANIMALS

› European Hare 44.7 mph
› Mountain Hare 43.5 mph
› Wolf 37-43.5 mph
› Fox 31-37 mph
› Moose, about 31 mph
› Wild boar, like a moose but short distances
› Roe deer, like a moose
› Brown bear 28 mph
› Badger 15.5-18.6 mph
› Housefly almost 5 mph

How far can a squirrel jump?

Imagine being a squirrel sitting on the branch of a spruce and getting ready to jump. You raise and lower your head up and down and look carefully at the branch you are aiming for. When you move your head this way, it is easier to judge the distance.

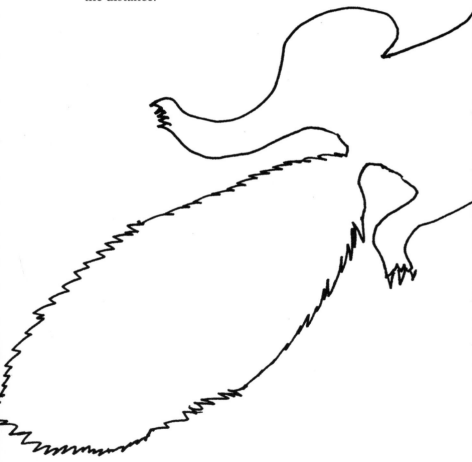

The squirrel standing still on its branch and moving its head quickly up and down is thinking and guessing how far away that other branch is. When it jumps straight out, it can go for about 4.9 feet before it starts falling down. If the squirrel fails to hit the branch it wants, it can handle falling down equally as far, before it lands on a branch closer to the ground. If the squirrel is being hunted, it can manage even longer jumps. Those are the moments when you can see it "fly" 32 to 39 feet and then quickly run off without having hurt itself. But jumps like that are rare to catch a glimpse of.

As the squirrel jumps it extends its legs and arms almost straight out in all directions. That way the stomach and arms create a larger gliding surface that makes it fly longer in the air. The squirrel also uses its tail to control its direction and keep its balance.

Did you know that...

...a normal sized grasshopper can jump about 10 feet if it stretches out its wings and glides?

... grasshoppers normally do not fly? The pink-winged grasshopper, *Bryodema tuberculata*, is an exception and it can fly hundreds of feet.

... Roe deers and hares do not have any collarbones? Animals that run and jump a lot need the most possible mobility in the front legs and because of this the shoulder blades cannot be attached to the rest of the body.

...the hedgehog is great at climbing? Hedgehogs have been seen to climb fences over 6.5 feet high!

... the Common Swift is the bird that spends the most time in the air? From the day the bird leaves its nest it flies nonstop for about 310, 685 miles until it lands to nest for the first time, two years later.

... the Common Swift has such weak legs that it needs help to gain air under its wings if it lands on the ground?

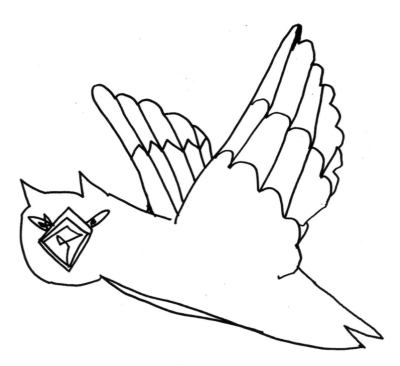

Arctic Terns that nest in the Arctic Ocean and then fly to the other end of the earth to "hibernate" in Antarctica make a journey of about 24,850 miles!

Snow Geese nest on the tundra in Siberia, amongst other places. When they move south some individuals fly over the highest tops of Himalaya, more than 26,246 feet above sea level.

Rüppell's Vultures and Cinereous Vultures are known for flying high. A Rüppell's Vulture probably holds the record for highest flying; a Rüppell's Vulture almost caused a catastrophe as it was caught in a jet engine of an airplane 37,073 feet up in the air.

RECORD-BREAKING EAGLE

Just like other birds, Golden Eagles use a few different methods to fly. When it flies under certain conditions, or rather glides downwards, it can reach a speed of almost 80 mph. A Golden Eagle in Scotland was clocked flying at a speed of 118 mph when bullied by a Peregrine Falcon, but the numbers are uncertain. The average speed for regular horizontal flight varies from about 28 to 31 mph.

LISTEN, MAKE NOISE, SEE, AND GLOW

Do grasshoppers have ears on their stomach?

Yes, as a matter of fact they do! Grasshoppers' hearing organs are placed on either side of the first rear body segment, or the "stomach." Katydids and crickets have their ears placed on either side of the front shin bone, just under the knee.

Most land-dwelling animals that make sounds have ears and can hear well. Well-developed hearing organs can be found on insects that produce sound for their own purposes, for example grasshoppers, katydids, and cicadas.

Many insects react to sound waves without having a specific hearing organ. Especially low tones can create vibrations in solid objects, for example an insect body. The vibrations are perceived through sensory cells that can be found in

Johnston's organ. This organ is placed in the antennae, and it is formed to a greater or lesser degree depending on the insect. The Chironomidaes and the mosquitoes have the most well developed Johnston's organ.

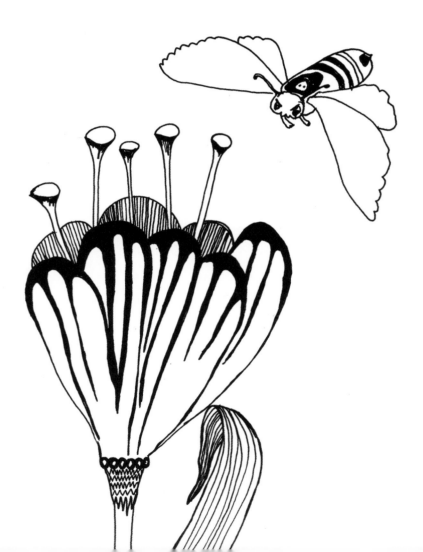

Insects buzz, rustle, snap, and make other sounds in different ways. In most cases the sound is a side effect that has no distinct purpose, sort of like the sound from an engine. However, some insects consciously produce sound to communicate. It can be used as a means of contact between sexes, like for example with grasshoppers and katydids, or with miscellaneous individuals as is the case with social insects like wasps and bees. In a few cases it is believed that the sound has a frightening effect, for example the Death's-head Hawkmoth's squeaking, chirping sound or the Apollo butterfly's rattling when you get too close to them.

A common way for insects to communicate is to rub two body parts against each other. One body part that is equipped with a row of small teeth, the so-called file or bow, is rubbed against a raised segment on another body part and it creates vibrations, the same way as when you pull your nails over a comb. On grasshoppers it is the thighs that act as bows and they are rubbed fast against a raised segment on the narrow and hard forewings. On katydids it is the left wing base that is the bow, and it is rubbed against the right wing base that has a rasp next to a crystal-clear membrane, the mirror. When the katydid wants to play it lifts its wings and moves them sideways so the bow is touching the rasp and the membrane starts swinging very fast.

GRASSHOPPER OR KATYDID?

Grasshoppers have short antennae, while katydids have very long antennae and are also usually bigger than grasshoppers.

Did you know that...

...a normal dog can perceive very high tones of up to 100,000 Hz? That is about five times higher than what a human can hear. They also have a better ability to sense lower frequencies.

...some wolf spider males court their females by drumming their abdomen against a surface? The females do not have any ears, but they can feel the vibrations.

...Fieldfares can hear the worms under the ground? To be able to better locate where the worm is digging through the soil they angle their head and ears toward the ground. Many people might believe that it is pure luck when the Fieldfares peck their beaks into the ground and pull up a long worm. But it's not the case!

...scared grass snakes smell bad? A frightened or excited grass snake can secrete smell through the skin and, if threatened, will empty the anal glands and cloaca of its stinky contents.

...that owls see with their ears when it is dark (but use their eyes when it is light enough)? Each opening for the ear has a different size and they are also somewhat different in height relative to each other. The ears are specially adapted to locate prey in three ways: in distance, sideways, and in height.

Why does the cat purr?

The cat does not only purr or spin to express that it is enjoying itself and feels well. It also purrs when it is frightened or worried, sometimes even when it is about to die and this is probably to calm itself. A new theory suggests that purring may have a healing and strengthening effect on the bones, by stimulating bone cells through the vibrations of their purring.

Animals that purr belong to the family of cats, *Felidae*, with its 42 species and the *Viverridae*, with its 66 species including the subfamily Paradoxurus, *Paradoxurinae*. But not all cats spin; the big cats—lion, tiger, leopard, jaguar, Snow leopard, Clouded leopard, and *Neofelis diardi*–do not spin. The puma is by definition a big cat and it can spin, but it is more closely related to the small cats than the big ones. The Eurasian lynx can also spin.

There are many theories about how the spinning or purring happens, and we do not know for sure how the cats are doing it. Probably the phenomenon is connected to the hyoid bone that can be found in the throat of small cats. Big cats have an elastic ligament instead of a bone.

BIRDS DO NOT HAVE ANY VOCAL CORDS

Birds do have a larynx but since it lacks vocal cords, the larynx cannot make any sound. The sounds are instead produced by *syrinx*, an enlargement of the larynx right where it splits into the two main bronchi, down in the chest cavity.

The syrinx has muscles and connective tissue made up of cartilage, and one or more vibration membranes that contribute to the production of sound. The cartilage is more or less converted fibrosis that is equivalent to the supportive fibrosis found in the larynx in mammals. Many birds have poorly developed syrinx muscles, for example storks, which explains why they are known for communicating by clattering with their beaks. Passerines, on the other hand, have a very well developed syrinx. Amongst these birds we can find many famous singing birds, like the Nightingale, Common Blackbird, and the Canary.

Since the syrinx is located below the larynx it is a part of the sound-producing apparatus, sort of like the pipe in a wind instrument. Because some birds have a substantially extended larynx and can make one or more notes, the similarity to a wind instrument then becomes even more striking. A long larynx allows the bird to produce lower tones. For example, the larynx of the Common Crane creates a double loop connected to the keel.

LATE SUMMER SINGING

After midsummer, birds usually become considerably quieter. It is because the struggle for females and the best territories is over, and the birds now have families. But it is not completely silent. There is still singing to be enjoyed from an occasional Chaffinch, Willow Warbler, Common Wood Pigeon, Blackcap, Eurasian Wren, or Blackbird. The birds singing at this time are partly males that did not succeed in mating yet, and partly males that want to start a second or third mating cycle.

Can moose see colors?

Moose, just like other species in the Cervidae family, are almost completely lacking the sensory cells, called cones, in the retina of the eye, which are essential for color vision. Moose are therefore almost entirely colorblind.

We can assume that moose experience their surroundings on a gray scale. Moose are, however, very good at detecting movement. The same goes for hedgehogs, which by the way have terrible vision. They can recognize contrasts of light against dark, but not objects. Although the hedgehog has poor vision, its sense of smell is excellent, and it is phenomenal at recognizing all sorts of smells. Its hearing is also very impressive.

Mammals' color vision is fairly well explored, but our knowledge of insect vision is minimal. Most of our facts are acquired from studies on the Western honey bee, and this knowledge has been transferred to other insects. It is well known that butterflies do not perceive colors the way we do. They also see colors that we cannot see, like ultraviolet light. Plants with nectar usually have bright colors and an entrance for insects in ultraviolet-colored patterns, to make themselves more attractive to nectar-eating insects.

Moths and other insects that are active at night are good at navigating by the starry night sky. But they are also attracted to the artificial light that humans invented. The dilemma here is that the sources of light created by humans are not infinitely far away, like the stars, but on the contrary within reach. When they get close to the actual source of light they become confused, maybe even blind, and do not know what to do. That is probably why they can be seen circling repeatedly around outdoor lights.

Examples of insects that are active at night and attracted to light are moths, caddies flies, chironomids, and other mosquitoes, some parasitoid wasps, European hornets, and some beetles. There are also birds that are attracted to light, for example Water Rail.

❊{ MYTH }❊

That bats are attracted to the color white is an old myth. Maybe the light surface attracts insects and thus also hungry bats. Or perhaps bats are just more easy to spot against a light background.

SOME OF THE MOST SENSITIVE ANIMALS

Bats have the best hearing and can also sense sounds that we cannot hear.

The Lobster Moth males, belonging to the family Notodontidae, have the best sense of smell. Male moths can smell a female moth several miles away.

Fish have the best sense of taste—they can actually find their way home by tasting the water. Imagine, eels might even feel the taste of their traditional mating place far away in the Sargasso Sea!

Birds of prey have the best vision. The Golden Eagle is said to be able to spot a hare from 9,840 feet. A Peregrine Falcon can see a dove from a distance of almost 5 miles.

Do self illuminating insects really exist?

Two species of insects that are self illuminating are the common glow-worm and the lesser glow-worm. Both are beetles, and the common glow-worm is (surprise!) more common.

It is in particular the female glow-worm that glows. She looks like a 1.1 inch-long gray-brown insect larva, but on the last two segments on the bottom of her abdomen there is a yellow colored area that light shines from. Usually the female is sitting still on a leaf a little bit above ground level and turns the tip of her abdomen so that the light is not blocked by the leaf. The light is yellow-green, similar to the type of light that burning phosphoric gives off. It is produced when the substance luciferin reacts with an enzyme causing it to oxidize to oxyluciferin. Almost all of the chemical energy is transformed into light, only about five percent is turned into heat.

The glow-worm male has wings and very large eyes. As a full-grown beetle he is about 0.5 inches long, with grey-brown elytra and a grey-yellow prothorax. He only glows weakly.

THE EUROPEAN ROBIN HAS MAGNETIC VISION

European Robins notice when the days get shorter and it is time to migrate. While moving south, they know how far they have gone by feeling the variations in the earth's magnetic fields. Now we also know that the magnetic field can affect the nutritional intake of birds. If you let the European Robin experience a magnetic field comparable to the one in the south of Spain, they will not gain the extra layer of fat that is needed for the long journey because the birds think they have already reached their destination. It is still unknown how the European Robin can feel the variations in the magnetic fields on earth.

How many degrees can an owl turn its head in each direction? 135° in each direction—in total three-quarters of one turn, 270°.

A PERSPECTIVE ON EGGS

Does the egg come out with the pointy or round end first?

———

The last part of the female bird's oviducts are rich in mucous glands; the secretions from these glands facilitate the egg's passage out of the body. This usually happens with the round end first, but not always. Penguin's eggs always come out with the pointy end first!

Different species's eggs look a little different. Over the course of evolutionary change, they have formed partly to come out of the body as painless as possible, and partly to be easy to hatch. Most eggs are more or less round, since it is likely the most practical shape. The Common Murre's eggs are sometimes left unattended on a narrow ledge, and since the egg is unevenly elongated it spins around its own axis when it lays by itself and cannot fall down from the narrow ledge.

Light, single-colored eggs are usually hidden in dark hollows. Species that lay their eggs in more visible areas often have speckled eggs, so that the eggs blend into the surroundings when the hatching bird leaves the nest. The unhatched eggs are safely camouflaged.

THE CHICK BREATHES THROUGH THE SHELL

The nutrition that the chick needs can be found inside of the egg but oxygen is taken up through pores in the shell. A regular egg from a hen contains nearly 10,000 of those pores. Through these microscopic "holes," oxygen comes in and carbon dioxide and water vapor go out. The chick is still not breathing with lungs, but receives oxygen through the fetal membranes, called the allantois. Blood from the fetus is circulating out to the allantois, where they takes up oxygen and lets out carbon dioxide.

At the pointy end of the egg is an air chamber between the two shell membranes. This chamber increases in size as water vapor from the growing chick evaporates from the egg. When the time for hatching is approaching, the chick pecks a hole in the air chamber and when it breathes in the air the lungs start working; at the same time it continues to receive oxygen through allantois. When it has finished pecking itself out of the egg shell, the baby bird begins to breathe using just its lungs.

REPTILES CANNOT HATCH

Birds and reptiles such as crocodiles and turtles are very closely related, and have similar eggs: The exchange of oxygen and carbon dioxide takes place in almost the same way. The major difference in the construction of the eggs is that reptiles do not have an air chamber. Another difference is how the eggs are kept warm: Since reptiles lack body heat of their own they have to rely on the sun to hatch their eggs, while the warm-blooded birds hatch without the same level of external heat.

Amphibians, on the other hand, lack fetal membranes in their eggs, which therefore have to be hatched in moist environments where the eggs can take up oxygen from the water. A few lizards, such as the Chalcides in Southern Europe and North Africa, have taken care of the fetuses' need for oxygen in an advanced way: Their fetuses are carried in the oviducts and receive oxygen through a variant of placenta that resembles the one that mammals have.

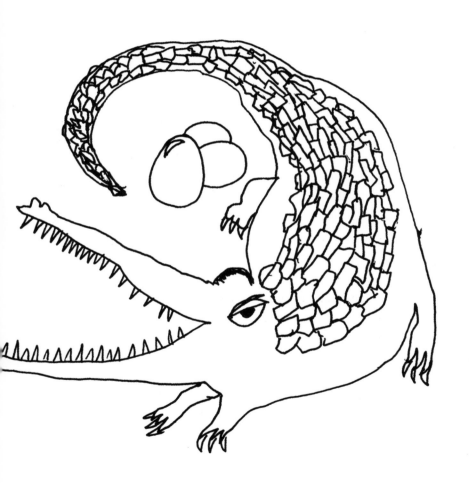

. . . the world's largest egg was laid by an ostrich in Borlänge? It weighed 5.5 pounds, which is equivalent to about 42 normal sized hen eggs.

. . . the world's smallest egg was laid by a hummingbird? It was less than 0.4 inches long and only weighed 0.014 ounces.

. . . spiders spin small silk sacs for their eggs? Some spiders leave the eggs to their fate, others carry around the sac until the eggs hatch. Other species then carry around the newly hatched babies until they are big enough to manage on their own, but in some cases the babies end up eating their mother.

. . . the Humpback whale lays five to seven eggs? However it is unusual that as many as five babies survive until the winter comes.

. . . Grass Snakes lay eggs once a year and it happens sometime between June and September? It then takes 5-10 weeks for the eggs to hatch.

. . . big eggs often have thinner shells than small eggs? That is because all egg shells contain almost the same amount of calcium, no matter what size they are. Usually young hens lay smaller eggs with thicker shells than the older hens do.

How do female birds produce enough lime to form a shell on the eggs?

Domesticated hens are often provided with supplementary lime, and we can assume that wild birds are skilled at finding sources of lime in nature. For example, female birds eat shells from snails but they have to be eaten at the right time, preferably on the night before the egg is about the be laid.

In the spring, you can provide birds with lime by laying out the shells from your breakfast eggs on the lawn! Blue Tits, Great Tits, Magpies, and other species will eat with great appetite. Birds can also keep extra supplies of calcium in their body in cavities in their skeleton. These extra supplies can then be released and used for producing eggshells.

D-hormone (vitamin D) has an important function in the birds' production of shells. Among other things, it is necessary for the ability to take up calcium from the intestines, and so that calcium can be released from the extra supplies in the skeleton. D-hormone exists in the body but it needs UV light from the sun to transform into the active form. It has been well known for a long time that birds in tropical areas (with shorter days) lay less eggs than birds in temperate regions (with longer days). To lay from 8 up to 16 eggs like our Great Tits would be nearly impossible in the tropics!

In nature birds usually lay eggs during a limited period of time, often in the spring, and then start hatching when the nest is full. But if the eggs are removed, the hen continues to lay. With domestic hens this behavior has been refined through breeding so that hens nowadays can lay one egg every day—all year round. But optimal nutrition and environment is necessary—the right light, temperature, and humidity—in order for it to work. With increased ability to lay eggs, the will to hatch is less, which means that commercial hens rarely manage to hatch chickens—if they get the chance to.

A LIVING PANTRY FOR THE BABIES

Mellinus arvensis is a wasp-like Sphecidae that is very common. When the female lays her eggs she first digs a pipeline cavity in the ground, 11-15 inches deep. Then she takes off hunting. She sneaks up to a fly or any other suitable prey and paralyzes it with her poison. When the fly has been subdued, she flies it to her cavity in the ground and pulls it down. The fly, still alive, is placed in a so called cell, and a fertilized egg is layered on top. Then she seals the cell and takes off hunting again. She continues this way until she has laid about 15 to 20 eggs in as many cells and the cavity is filled. As the eggs hatch the larvae eat their flies, and pupate over the winter. The year after, the new Sphecidaes are hatched.

55

ANIMALS THAT LAY EGGS AND HAVE AN INTERNAL FERTILIZATION SYSTEM

> All birds
> All insects, i.e. beetles, butterflies, flies, etc.
> All molluscs, i.e. snails, clams, octopuses, etc.
> Many reptiles, for example crocodiles, turtles, and snakes, but not the common European viper.
> All spiders and ticks.
> A few fish, for example sharks and rays.
> Three species of mammals: platypus and two spiny anteaters.

Maybe a few arthropods also have internal fertilization, since they mate, but it seems as if the fertilization itself takes place outside of the female body. The sperm is transferred through fluid or in the shape of so called spermatophore to the female, who keeps the semen in a capsule for some period of time; it's her decision when the eggs are going to be fertilized. The eggs are then hatched either as juveniles, which resemble the grown arthropod, or as larvae which pass through several different stages before it reaches adulthood.

A QUESTION OF AGE

Which animal lives the longest?

There are few facts about animals' maximum ages, and they are usually based on the lifespan of animals that lived in zoos. In nature, animals rarely become as old since they more often surrender to predatory animals, starvation, parasites or illness.

Amongst mammals, human beings live the longest with a maximum lifespan of 110 to 120 years. Apes do not become as old; the chimpanzee is said to live up to 40 or 50 years, and the gorilla about 50 years.

Generally mammals live longer the bigger they are. Humans are not typical since we live a very long time, relative to our bodyweight. The Indian Elephant is said to live up to 70 or 80 years in nature. The African Bush Elephant can get up to 60 years old, and the African Forest Elephant lives up to 80 years. There are no secure data about the big whales, but according to certain estimates they can live for more than 100 years. If this is true, there are many species of whale that compete with humans for being the mammal that lives the longest.

THE EYE CAN TELL

The accounts of having found harpoon blades of stone and ivory in today's Bowhead whales appears to be rather unbelievable. The Inuits stopped using that type of harpoon in the middle of the 1800s, which would have made these whales a lot more than 100 years old. The discovery of harpoons sparked scientists to try to determine the age of Bowhead whales by using age-related changes in the proteins that build the lens of the eye. Unlike most other proteins in the body these can not regenerate; the proteins the furthest back in the lens can thus be dated from when they were first formed in the fetus. When the eye lenses of a number of Bowhead whales killed within the years of 1978 and 1996 were studied, five whales were found to be older than 100 when they died. One of the whales was determined to be 211 years old, and could thereby be the oldest known mammal.

If we look at vertebrates, there are big tortoises that can live up to 150-200 years. From India there are accounts of a turtle that was captured in the Seychelles and lived for 255 years before it died in captivity. The most famous of all turtles, Lonesome George on the Galapagos Islands, however, only had an estimated age of 70-80 years. The gloomy name comes from being the last individual of his subspecies.

Animals (and plants) that reproduce asexually produce a common clone where every individual is almost genetically identical. It can therefore be claimed that a clone is an individual who could live forever. For example, Sweden's only reef forming coral, *Lophelia pertusa*, reproduces asexually by dividing itself. The reef in Kosterhavet National Park has been proven to be at least 8000 years old!

Bacteria and other microorganisms are similar. They do not age, but instead constantly split and generate new cells. They can therefore be said to live an eternity. In other words, aging is only something that exists in multicellular organisms with sexual reproduction.

How long does a butterfly live?

The answer depends on how you count. The life of a butterfly starts with the egg and continues with a number of caterpillar stages and then on to the pupa stage, and finally reaches the end-stage, the full-grown butterfly. If you count that way most butterflies live for about one year.

Some butterfly species have time for several generations during one season and then live a considerably shorter life. That goes for the *Macroglossum stellatarum* that we can see when autumn comes and that probably are hatched from eggs of butterflies that came here from the Mediterranean in June-July. They die the very same autumn and have a lifespan of only two months in total.

It should also be mentioned that several species have a lifespan of two years or longer, for example many species that live a harsh and difficult life on moors or similar places. Some species can live as a pupa for a very long time, the Small Eggar for up to nine years!

LIFE CYCLE OF THE SMALL TORTOISESHELL

The Small Tortoiseshell belongs to one of the species that hibernates as a full-grown butterfly. When the overwintering area is warming up in the spring, hibernation is interrupted and the butterflies start looking for a suitable partner. After mating, the female lays her eggs on young nettles. The eggs are hatched after a week and the larvae eat the nettles. The larval development that takes place before pupating lasts for two to three weeks, and the pupa stage then lasts for one up to two weeks. The full-grown butterflies are hatched at the end of June and all the way into August.

Newly born butterflies quickly find flowers rich in nectar and there they fuel themselves for a couple of weeks. After that they go back to their overwintering areas, a cavity in a tree or the ground, an outdoor basement, or simply on a tree or a branch. They do this whether or not it is cold or it stays warm outside. Here they settle down to rest with their wings folded together in an upside-down position until next spring.

. . . a wolverine?
In captivity it can live for 16-18 years but there is no proof of how old it can get in its wild habitat.

. . . a salmon?
The data varies from 13 to 15 years.

. . . a woodpecker?
The highest known age for a Great Spotted Woodpecker is 12 years and 8 months.

. . . an earthworm?
Since earthworms live under the ground they are very difficult to study. According to reports our common earthworm, *Lumbricus terrestris*, lives 5-6 years.

. . . a bat?
If the bat survives its first winter it can live up to 20-30 years old. However a great number of the babies, more than half, die during their first year of life.

. . . a tick?
A normal female tick lives between 2 and 6 years.

. . . a hedgehog?
Up to 19 years.

. . . a cat?
According to The Guinness Book of World Records, a domesticated cat can live up to 34 years.

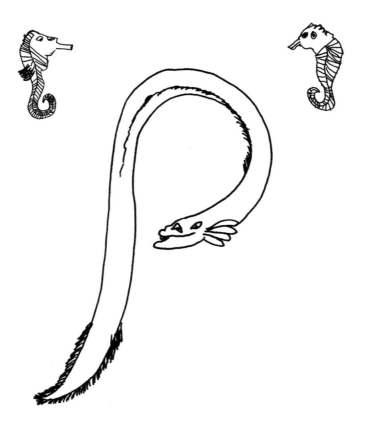

Putte from Helsingborg is the longest living eel that has been documented. He was captured in 1836 and at that point had an estimated age of three years. He was kept in captivity at the Helsingborg museum until he died in 1948, at 88 years old. In a wild habitat eels are said to live for 50-55 years. There are also a great deal of unconfirmed rumors with unknown accuracy. One stubborn rumor was circulating in the media at the beginning of the 1960s, of an eel in a well in the Scanian Brantevik that was said to have lived for 103 years.

FOOD AND DRINKS

How many cones does a squirrel peel and eat in one day?

The squirrel has a built-in "nutcracker" in the form of teeth made for gnawing that constantly grow. It can open cones by quickly chopping off every cone leaf and then catching the two seeds found next to it.

To eat a spruce cone takes an average of seven minutes for the squirrel, while a pine cone can be eaten in only three minutes. But *how many* cones a squirrel can eat is more difficult to know. Squirrels at a research center ate seeds from about 30 spruce cones each day, even if the variation was great. Many factors affect the intake of cones; for example, squirrels eat less if it is windy, rainy, or cold and snowy. Squirrels strongly dislike cones that are sticky with resin, so if they find many they'll seek out another tree with less sticky cones.

If you are in the woods and are watching a squirrel peel cones, it may happen that the squirrel starts swishing its tail back and forth, smacking its paws together, and jumping so that its claws make noise against the tree bark (it can be heard from a distance of several hundred feet in a quiet forest). This is the way squirrels communicate to other squirrels that there is danger nearby. Maybe it saw you and was frightened and thought you were disrupting, or it saw something else it considered as a threat. For example a Northern Goshawk, a hawk that likes to eat squirrels. If the squirrel manages to see the hawk before it sees the squirrel, it stays very quiet and freezes to stay undiscovered. Generally it sits that way for up to ten minutes before it becomes active again.

Did you know that . . .

. . . the most important food for the squirrel during autumn and winter are seeds from spruce and pine cones, as well as hazelnuts when they can be found. Spruce and pine cones are very rich in protein and fats, and also contain several important minerals.

Do fish drink water?

The question can be answered in a few different ways depending on the fish's environment. The fish adapt in different ways depending on whether they live in freshwater, salt water, or brackish water.

"Simple" fish like the Atlantic Hagfish have a similar concentration of salt in their bodily fluids, as the surrounding water. Sharks and rays, on the other hand, have a *lower* concentration compared to the surrounding water. Their method to even out the concentration of salt in their body is complicated. The method does however not necessitate that the fish drink; it is an internal regulation.

Freshwater bony fish, for example perch or pike, have a *higher* concentration of salt in their bodily fluids compared to the surrounding water. The result is that water is constantly going in through the skin and the gills. Consequently they continuously have to get rid of water and they do this through highly effective kidneys that produce diluted urine. They also lose water through the gill membranes.

COD AND MACKEREL ARE DOING IT!

Salt water bone fish like cod and mackerel have a salinity level that is lower than the surrounding water. Therefore they tend to lose water through the skin and gills, and they must replace the water that has been lost at the same speed. Therefore they have developed mechanisms and behavior to compensate for the loss of water; for example, their kidneys are specially modified. Drinking alone would not be enough. The intake of water is aided by specialized stages in the digestive system.

Why do butterflies not burn on nettles?

The Small Tortoiseshell is one of our most common butterflies. It lays its eggs on our nettles and the larvae that are born live off nettles. But why don't they get burned?

The stinging hairs on nettles are hollow and connected to a small sac of venom. The hairs are very fragile and break even at the slightest touch. Their tip then breaks at an angle and operates as a thin needle when the venom sac is emptied. How the Tortoiseshell larvae manage to not break the stinging hairs and be hurt by the sharp edges is still a mystery. One possibility is that they are immune to the poison, but it seems more likely that they somehow manage to not break the stinging hairs.

The nettles' equal among animals, the jellyfish, does not have many enemies. However there is one fish that does not hesitate in front of the burning jellyfish tentacles—the lumpsucker. It eats not only jellyfish, but also small arthropods, polychaetes, and small fish.

POISONOUS NECTAR

It is worse for bumblebees that eat poisonous nectar. Every year, especially around midsummer, dead or dying bumblebees and bees are found on the ground under linden trees. The cause of this is not confirmed. According to some scientists, the insects die from natural toxins in the pollen of the linden tree called saponins, which dissolve red blood cells. Other scientists believe the nectar of some linden trees contains the sugar mannose that bees and bumblebees cannot digest. They then die from starvation even though they are full of food. Why some linden trees produce mannose is unknown. Another, but maybe not very likely, theory is that a process in the bee's intestine transforms linden nectar to a poisonous substance.

SPEAKING OF

Insects can never grow fat because they have an outer skeleton made from hard chitin, the shape of which does not change. Insect larvae, on the other hand, can become rather fat. The abdomen can get enormously swollen, not because they are fat, but because the females carries the eggs.

How does the spider's digestive system work?

The digestive process of spiders takes place both internally and externally. The spider injects its poison in the prey through canals in their jaws. The poison is usually adapted to what prey the spider has caught, and if it is supposed to kill or paralyze the prey.

The poison starts the process of breaking down the prey to liquid, because spiders can only eat fluids. Then the spider sucks up the melted guts. During the meal the prey is usually in a cocoon.

Despite its poison, spiders are mostly known for the noble art of spinning webs. All spiders can spin, but not all can make webs. The family of orb-weavers, to which the European Garden Spider, *Araneus diadematus,* belongs, spins the characteristic and most well recognized wheel-like net. The sticky threads of the catch and hold flying prey for a while until the garden spider, who often is waiting in a spun hiding place at the edge of the net, registers the kicking catch through vibrations in the thread. The spider then quickly rushes over, spins a cocoon around the prey, and kills it or paralyzes it with its poison. The web has both sticky and dry threads, which allow the spider to walk only on the dry threads and not get stuck like his prey.

Similar webs for catching prey are made by a large number of spider species. Usually the net is constructed so that you, with some practice, can learn to see what species made the web.

Where do fruit flies come from?

—

We have all experienced how fruit flies pop up from nowhere. They gather in leftovers of apples, fruit peels, and overripe fruit to eat and reproduce.

If the weather is warm and you happen to have left overripe fruit in the kitchen, it easily attracts fruit flies and other small flies that are dependent on fruit. The females lay their eggs in the pulp, where there is no risk of them drying out. But there is not much oxygen; the egg, which is about 0.02 inches long, therefore has two outgrowths for breathing—"gills"—that stick out into the air and help it to absorb oxygen. Soon the egg hatches into a little larva that starts to eat the pulp. When it has grown for a few days, it becomes an immobilized pupa. After another few days, a full-grown fruit fly is hatched from the pupa. Since all the stages from mating to becoming a sexually mature fly only take about ten days in optimal conditions, the fruit flies can multiply rapidly.

The small fruit flies are most common in the summer but can also show up other times of the year in fruit that we carry home from the grocery store. The risk is particularly big with unconventional fruit. The fruit fly larvae can also live in fluids like wine and beer. The pupation then takes place on the inside of the container, above the liquid surface. If you leave wine in open containers to make vinegar you can be sure to attract these flies. That is why they sometimes are called vinegar flies.

HOW TO GET RID OF THE FLIES

Mix one part water, one part apple cider vinegar, and a few drops of dishwashing liquid (to remove the surface tension) in a glass and place it on the sink. In a few days the fruit flies will have gathered in the glass and you do not have to deal with them buzzing around you!

Did you know that...

...the fruit fly is one of the best animals for geneticists to experiment on? The reason is partly that the flies have such a short generation time, and partly because the salivary glands in full-grown larvae have so-called giant chromosomes that are easy to study.

HUNTING BEHAVIOUR OF ...

...antlions?

Antlions are predators that live in sand. They throw away the sand so that a funnel-shaped pitfall is created and then stay at the bottom waiting for ants and other small insects to fall down. The antlions use their powerful and hollow jaws to hold and drain their victims.

...Common Buzzard?

Common Buzzards do eat snakes, but their most common prey is voles and mice. They have three different ways of hunting: the most common is to sit on a lookout, for example on telephone poles, dead trees, or high rocks. From there they dive towards their prey.

In other cases they glide about 320 feet over open terrain and dive on their prey when they have discovered it. Often they have to continue to hunt the prey for a while on the ground.

77

. . . *Roe deer?*

Roe deer are real connoisseurs and carefully select their food. They have to pick high quality food at the right time of the year. They need to be so careful because roe deer cannot handle food with too much fiber in it. The food has to be easy to digest and full of nutrition. It is best that they eat berry bushes, for example blueberry and lingonberry, but heather as well. Since the range of plants varies during the year, their diet differs depending on season. In the spring the first growing straws of grass are very popular, and the so called garden Roe deer are very fond of allioideae, a subfamily of flowering plants. In the summer, the Roe deer eat a lot of herbs and leaves, and in the autumn they prefer mushrooms when they are available, otherwise berry bushes. Ripe oats and wheat can be tempting too, but not rye or barley! In the winter the berry bushes are important, but if the snow is covering the ground they eat a great deal of needles mostly from pine, but sometimes spruce, which they don't like as much.

. . . *pikes?*

Pikes eat most things that pass by, including ducklings, frogs, snakes, and crayfish. The latter are their favorite, and the hard shell is not a problem for the pike to digest. There are reports of a pike caught recently that had three large crayfish, each about 2.7 inches long, in its stomach!

. . . *butterflies?*

Most common with grown butterflies is that they suck or drink a sugary solution (nectar) from flowers but some of them do not eat at all. Butterfly larvae mostly eat different parts of plants.

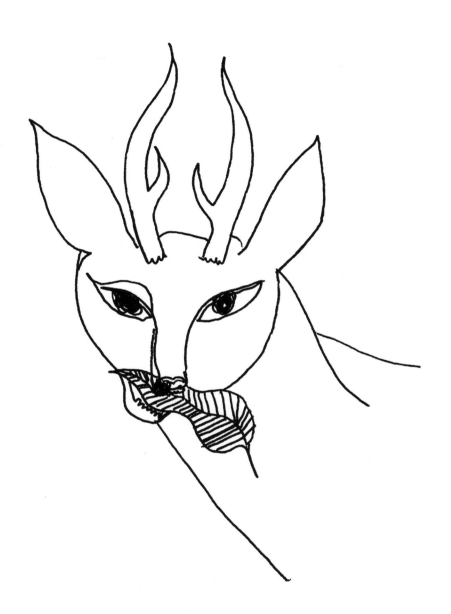

. . . ladybugs?
The majority of ladybugs are predators, both as larvae and as full-grown beetles. They mostly eat plant lice and scale insects, but sometimes they can be seen drinking the nectar from a flower.

. . . ground beetles?
Both larvae and full-grown insects are mainly predators that are very active in their hunt for prey, for example earthworms, insects, or small snails.

. . . grasshoppers?
Grasshoppers mainly eat grass, and the same goes for katydids who also eat seeds and different small animals.

WHY ARE BIRD DROPPINGS WHITE?

Birds have a single body orifice for feces and urine as well as reproductive waste, called a cloaca. The urine gathers in the cloaca where the fluids are absorbed back into the blood. The final product is then a semi solid light mass of uric acid—bird droppings.

✥{ MYTH }✥

No, flies do not "taste" food when they rub one leg against the other. Just like us, they have their gustatory system in the mouth. They are most likely cleaning themselves and rubbing off little particles that stick to their legs and wings. To be able to fly as fast as possible it is important to keep weight down.

WINTER—SLEEP AND COLD

Do flys sleep even though they don't have any eyelids?

No, flies do not sleep. They do lack eyelids, but that is not the reason why they do not sleep. Just like humans need sleep, the flies need inactive periods; they then sit completely still and try not to be seen.

Sleep is a recurring, spontaneous state with impaired ability to react to outer stimuli. In other words it is a form of rest. All higher animals down to reptiles, as well as a few fish species, sleep regularly.

Hibernation is a special type of sleep. Hibernation is a state of inactivity during a long period of time, usually with reduced life functions. During hibernation body temperature drops close to the temperature of the surrounding climate.

As a result, the animal's metabolism is considerably reduced and the body's need for energy is much less. Hibernation therefore saves energy—it is cheap to hibernate and live sparingly on the fat stored from a period of good food supplies. Real hibernation occurs with big and medium sized animals.

THE HEDGEHOG ALMOST QUITS BREATHING

In order for the hedgehog to make it through winter it has to lower its body temperature and thus reduce its metabolic rate considerably. It hibernates rolled up in a special den for the winter, under a pile of leaves or dug down in a compost pile of dirt, or similar places.

The body temperature sinks low (37-42°F) and breathing is reduced from the summer's 40-50 breaths per minute to as few as 6-9 per minute. The heart rate is also dramatically reduced. This conservation of energy makes it possible for the hedgehog to manage six months of hibernation without eating.

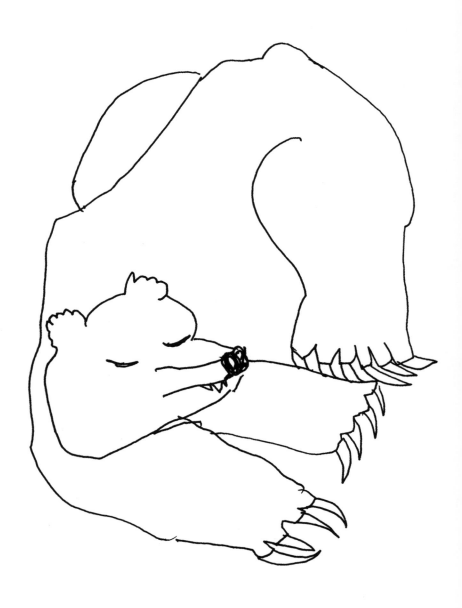

Do bears pee in their dens?

No, bears do not need to pee when they are hibernating. If they did they would have a problem with the balance of fluids in their body, since bears neither drink or eat during hibernation.

The only water that bears lose in hibernation is the air that they breath out. But it is replaced with water that is produced when fat decomposes through the process of burning fat, and that keeps the bear from being thirsty. Under normal circumstances when the bear is *not* hibernating, uric acid and other harmful nitrogen compounds are produced in the body and then released through pee. When the bear is hibernating the nitrogen compounds are absorbed into the blood where they are broken down by bacteria and therefore are not necessary to pee out. During the winter rest, other important bodily functions stop—the bear neither eats, drinks, or poops.

THE BEAR IS ONLY SLEEPING

The bear's winter rest is not a real hibernation, since it only lowers its body temperature by a few degrees. If the bear lowered its body temperature as much as, for example, the hedgehog, it would save a lot of energy and thus not need to "fatten up" as much before winter rest.

So why don't bears hibernate? The answer is that the heating time after the hibernation would be too long. It would take about one day to heat the big body from 41°F to 98.6°F and the process would use up a lot of energy.

It is not only bears that rest in the wintertime. Bats hibernate, since there is no food for them. When nights in the autumn start getting cold, they seek out their hibernation spots. During hibernation, the body temperature drops to the same as the surrounding temperature and the bodily functions run on low energy. Bats can wake up a few times during the winter, to change position or drink water. But they cannot wake too often since it drains the animal's fat reserves. A sleeping bat should therefore not be disturbed during wintertime.

Badgers also sleep through the winter.

BATS REST UPSIDE DOWN

When landing, many bats turn their head downwards when already in the air, so that they can comfortably attach their bottom feet in a resting position. Hanging upside down is the most common way to sleep but not the only one. Some individuals can sometimes be found sleeping horizontally; for example, in the crack of a rock. The reason that they mostly hang is probably because they have a hard time lifting off from a flat surface when they are about to fly off. To hang upside-down makes it easier to just let go and start flying immediately. Their way of hanging so closely together is likely due to lack of space.

What about fish in the wintertime?

When the water temperature sinks, the fish's body temperature sinks as well since they are cold blooded. Their metabolic rate runs on low speed, since they do not use a lot of energy and thus do not need to eat as often. But as all ice fishermen know, the perch bites also in the wintertime!

Fish are not likely to get cold. Even if they can feel differences in temperature, the cooling process is so slow that they probably do not even notice it. Since they are cold blooded their body temperature adapts to the surrounding temperature. Most fish however have a temperature minimum; some tropical species die at 59°F. The most extreme fish can stand 28°F (!) and lives in the Antarctic.

Considering how common a material water is, it has many unusual characteristics. One of them is that water is the heaviest at 39.2°F, which means that warmer as well as colder water floats on top. Another unusual characteristic is that ice also floats. That is why lakes and other water currents deeper than 3 to 6.5 feet normally do not freeze at the bottom. If they did, there are many species that would die because of lack of oxygen. A strange exception is the crucian carp who can live even in frozen water in the wintertime.

1. The koala: 22 hours per day. It can be compared to a newborn baby, who sleeps about 16 hours.

2. Sloths: 20 hours.

3. Armadillos and opossums: 19 hours.

4. Lemur: 16 hours.

5. Hamster and squirrel: 14 hours.

Did you know that...

...whales sleep in two different ways? Either they rest calmly in a horizontal or vertical position in the water, or they sleep slowly swimming next to another whale.

...dolphins only sleep with one brain half at a time? In this state they are less receptive of their surroundings and often only swim in circles.

...one of the major unsolved mysteries of science is sleep? We have to sleep but nobody knows why. Humans are not the only creatures that sleep; animals all the way down to at least flies also need to sleep.

BIRDS DO NOT GET COLD

Birds have veins deep inside their legs that work as heaters and prevent loss of heat through the feet. That way they can stand still on ice without being cold. When the temperature sinks under about 14°F you can see how they lower their whole body over the feet, which also helps with staying warm.

INSECTS CAN WAKE UP

Most insects rest as pupae in the wintertime, but there are also those who rest as full grown insects. As soon as the weather starts getting milder and the temperature reaches 30°F, these can wake up from their winter rest. Some are specially adapted to a colder climate, for example winter crane flies.

Amongst butterflies there are a few species that rest like larvae in the winter, usually hairy ones. But even these can wake up in temporary mild weather and crawl off on the snow. The unmistakable fox moth, hairy and brown and up to about 4 inches long, survives even if it is frozen inside the snow or ice!

The peacock butterfly, like some other butterflies, is adapted to winter resting as a full-grown butterfly. If you find a butterfly awake in the winter you can try to put it in a dark and cool place, which gives it a great chance of surviving until it is time for it to be outside and fly. You should not give it anything to "eat."

Are there butterflies that migrate?

Birds' habit of migrating is a well known phenomena. When cold weather strikes in the autumn they fly south. Then they return the next spring or summer to nest, since there is more food and space around here. But what about butterflies?

The fact that insects also migrate might not be very well known. The Red Admiral, for example, leaves the heat in North Africa in the spring or early summer and flies up to more northern latitudes. This migration might be because there are too many individuals of the same species or that the food supplies for the larvae is not enough, and so some of them—sometimes all of them—are forced to migrate.

The Admiral Butterfly usually comes here in June. The female lays egg on nettles, the larvae hatch and live off of the nettle leaves until it is time to pupate. The new butterflies are then hatched during the summer. When the days get shorter we can notice a certain pattern of butterflies moving south. That means it is not the migrated individuals that move south, but the next generation.

IS
IT
DANGEROUS?

SNAKES AND OTHER POISONOUS CREATURES

When are you the least likely to get bitten by a viper?

The common European viper is cold blooded and has varying body temperature depending on how cold or warm the surrounding environment is. An easier way to put it is: the warmer it gets, the more ready they are to strike!

In cold conditions or in cloudy weather the snakes mostly keep still. By being exposed to the warming rays of the sun they can increase their body temperature and their metabolic rate and they become more agile. The viper's activity is therefore controlled by the surrounding temperature, which means that the risk of being bitten is greater when it is warm and sunny but lesser when it is cloudy and cold.

Snakes can be found almost everywhere except in very urban areas. Despite this you rarely meet them, since snakes prefer keeping away from us rather than risking confrontation.

SNAKE IN THE COMPOST? CONGRATULATIONS!

To have a snake in your garden has its advantages—you will not have problems with voles and mice. In springtime the snakes temporarily visit gardens when moving from their winter rest to summer territory. They quickly move along. If you have snakes around the house later in the season it can be assumed that they live on or near the property.

To lower the risk of permanent snakes in your garden you should make the area as unwelcoming as possible for them. Start by removing piles of sticks and cairns, seal eventual cavities in stone walls and house foundations, check basement ventilators for nests, keep the grass short and see to it that composts and piles of leaves are not too close to your house. Try to disturb the snakes as much as possible without hurting them. For example you can stomp around near them.

If you succeed in chasing off the snake's prey you can be fairly sure that you will not have a snake in your garden for a very long time. Sometimes you hear that tobacco can scare off snakes. It is true that snakes shun tobacco; at least they are very sensitive to nicotine. But even if you could afford to lay a string of tobacco around your property it would be washed away by the rain, as well as pose a risk of poisoning other animals.

98

SNAKES ARE ENDANGERED

In Sweden there are three species of snakes: viper and grass snakes, which are both common, and the southern and rare smooth snake. All Swedish snakes are endangered. According to law it is forbidden to kill, harm, capture, or in any other way collect a wild living specimen of any Swedish snake. It is, however, permitted to capture and relocate living vipers when they are found on your property. But neither the grass snake or smooth snake can be touched.

Did you know that...

... if a poisonous snake bites another poisonous snake of the same species, nothing happens? A viper is in other words resistant to its own poison.

... vipers are excellent swimmers?

... snakes themselves cannot dig but like to use voles' passages and other already existing burrows?

✳{MYTH}✳

"If you place a real absinthe wormwood by the front door no snakes will come into your house." Unfortunately this is only an old tale. The person who finds a herb that actually works is encouraged to contact the On Duty Biologist!

IF YOU GET BITTEN—CONTACT A DOCTOR!

Around 200 people are hospitalized yearly due to being bitten by a viper. Between 20 to 30 percent of them have moderate to severe symptoms. The reaction after being bit by a viper varies a lot depending on how much poison you have in you. In almost half of the cases no symptoms will occur, which is because no poison was injected. Usually you see two small marks 0.02 to 0.03 inches apart from each other.

It is highly unusual for humans to die from snake bites. But the poison from the viper can be dangerous for a hypersensitive person. The poison control centers recommend persons bit by a snake to contact a doctor.

HAVE IN MIND

. . . that suitable shoes or boots can protect against snake bites. Most people get bitten in the foot or ankle.

. . . never pick up snakes.

✦{ MYTH }✦

"If you are bitten by a viper baby in the spring, you will die within two days if you are not treated." The most poisonous snakes are not the little babies, but the biggest snakes since these have the most venom.

SNAKE OR LIZARD?

The little slow-worm can easily be mistaken for being a snake since it does not have any legs and also moves like a snake. But it is, in fact, a lizard. Slow-worms are different from snakes because they have eyelids and blink like other lizards, their ear opening is visible and they shed their skin in many pieces instead of just one like snakes do. Underneath the body the slow-worm has small scales—just like they have on top of the body. Snakes have (almost always) extra large and wide scales under the body.

Are there poisonous fish in Sweden?

There are a variety of tales about the the toxicity of fish: The ruffe has toxic mucus, the zander has toxic blood, the perch has poisonous dorsal fins and the weever has toxic thorns on its operculums. Sure proof can only be found about the weever's toxicity.

The ruffe is said to have toxic mucus, but probably all fish mucus has some sort of antibacterial function. The perch supposedly has toxic dorsal fins which is doubtful, although it could be considered that the thorns, like other sharp objects, can give secondary infections. The claim that the zander would have toxic blood is entirely unsupported.

But the weever's toxicity is quite well documented. This little fish has a toxic thorn on each operculum and all the spines in the front dorsal fin are toxic. The thorns and their poison are only used in self defense and not when hunting preys. When the fish feels threatened the operculums flip out and the front dorsal fin is raised. The thorns are thick and can pierce through thinner materials and also human skin. The operculum thorns as well as the spine contain a white glandular tissue. After an injection of poison the thorn in question is immediately filled up again. Note that even dead fish have poison in their thorns.

Accidents often occur when the fish is being removed from the net but it sometimes happens that a swimmer accidentally steps on the fish. The poison causes a local reaction with immediate intense pain, swelling and discoloration of skin. Untreated pain can last for a day. The swelling can last for weeks and in rare cases months. Symptoms of headache, dizziness, chills, sweating, and nausea occur. Bacterial infection can occur as a complication.

Is it possible to die from a jellyfish?

There are jellyfish that are extremely toxic, such as the infamous box jellyfish, which has killed roughly 5,500 people since 1954, when records were first kept for jellyfish fatalities.

Along the Swedish west coast the moon jelly, lion's mane jellyfish, blue jellyfish, compass jellyfish and the barrel jellyfish are naturally occurring species. In the Baltic sea there is only the moon jelly. Compass jellyfish, blue jellyfish and the lion's mane jellyfish almost always only cause local symptoms, in the shape of a burn-like skin irritation.

In tropical countries there are considerably more toxic species. Some of these are the Portuguese Man o' War, box jellyfish and the Irkudanji jellyfish. These jellyfish, also known as "stingers," are each year involved in serious incidents with severe poisoning, and can even cause deaths.

DEFENSE OR ATTACK?

When it comes to toxic animals there are two types: those who use their venom as a defense against attackers and those who use it to kill prey and get food. For animals in the sea the venom works as a defense function for most species while the animals on land often use the venom as both a tool of defense and an attacking weapon.

OUR FRIENDS WITH A STING

How many stripes does a wasp have?

It is possible to say that female wasps have twelve stripes—six black and six yellow—while the males have fourteen stripes. The number varies greatly, however. In Sweden we have twelve species of social wasps and they all look a little different from each other.

All wasps have a rear body that generally is striped in yellow and black. Usually there is at least a yellow part and a black part on the rear body segment, even if they are not always in straight lines. The black parts (which sometimes are in the shape of dots) are always closest to the middle body segment but can sometimes be completely missing, so that the rear body looks yellow. However the rear body can sometimes be almost completely black, especially in north of Sweden where the black pigments can overtake the yellow. Black wasps are a rather organic adjustment to the colder climate: Wasps are cold blooded animals that need to be heated by the sun and the black color makes the body temperature rise faster.

STOP WAVING YOUR ARMS!

The best advice to avoid being stung is to act normally and not wave your arms around the wasps. Think of how wasps actually are useful beings! Since they are predators they catch different kinds of insect larvae as food for their own larvae. That way they keep troublesome pests away from berry bushes and fruit trees, and are very useful in our gardens. Wasps are not nectar specialists, but find all sorts of plants with easily accessible nectar, so they are quite good pollinators.

If you still do not want wasps around you it is wise to remove old nests during the winter. Wasps do not reuse their old nests and it is unlikely females will hibernate in it, but they do like to build a new one that is connected to the old one. Therefore make sure to fill any cavities, so the wasps cannot return to the same place next summer. There are also purely sanitary reasons to clean out old nests; the leftovers from the old one can attract skin beetles and other pests we do not want around us.

Wasps are predators and therefore like everything we eat—meat, fish, seafood, and other food rich in protein. Vegetables, on the other hand, they will not eat. Wasps need fluid, and they drink nectar that is found in most plants' flowers. The nectar is sugary, and therefore wasps are attracted to anything that is sweet. This is why you should not let fruit fallen from trees lay around your garden.

> › Only serve vegetarian food and only drink ice water
> › Avoid deodorant, cologne, and perfume
> › Do not wear Hawaiian shirts, or dresses and blouses with flower patterns
> › Avoid sudden movements, waving, and strikes
> › Do not stay close to a wasp's nest. Most of all do not sit on or close to the nest entrance path
> › Do not be afraid! If you are scared you will send out alarm pheromones that can attract wasps

SMALL BUMBLEBEES CAN ALSO STING

Just like bees and wasps, bumblebees have a stinger connected to a venom sac. Just like regular bees, bumblebees will sting if they are annoyed. The bumblebee poison has a burning effect, which is why you say that bumblebees burn.

There are a number of differences between bumblebees and bees: Bumblebees fly in lower temperatures, even at 50°F, while bees need at least 53.5°F to be able to fly. That means that bumblebees are up earlier in the morning

and later at night compared to bees. Bumblebees, on the other hand, fly shorter distances and thus have a smaller territory. This is likely one of the reasons that bumblebees have been proven to be better at pollinating greenhouses than bees. Bumblebees also lack the ability to inform other individuals within their own community of a good source of nutrition. Some bumblebee species have longer tongues than bees and can therefore also drink from flowers with nectar deep inside, such as red clover.

Is it possible to predict a wasp filled summer?

As an On Duty Biologist, I often receive questions of a predicting nature, like: Will there be many wasps this year? Of course it is hard to tell how the year will turn out, but it is possible to try to make a somewhat qualified guess.

Last year's conditions can usually give you clues: If the late summer was cold and rainy, there is a high chance that many wasp communities collapsed and went under. There was no time to hatch very many productive offspring, since it is not until the late summer that the fertile males and females are hatched. Earlier in the season only sterile workers have been hatched, which help to build the nest, find nectar, and in other ways make it nice for others that live in the community.

When the reproducers mate the male dies. But the female, also known as the queen, finds a place safe from cold to rest over the winter. Of the old society, everyone dies except the females that have mated to pass on the species to next year. Mild winters with few and short periods of cold are favorable to the hibernating queens. Humid weather also produces a risk of mold.

A disastrous late summer and winter period can however be followed by an unusually favorable spring and early summer. Lots of sun, heat, and suitable food can make it possible for the nests that have survived, against the odds, to thrive and evolve beyond all expectations. That is when all the predictions fail. It is not easy to always be right but at least you can do your best!

Did you know that...

. . . the wasp sting lacks barbs and therefore stays on the wasp after it has stung? In other words it can sting several times. The honey bee's sting has barbs and gets stuck on whoever is stung. Therefore the honey bee can only sting once, and dies thereafter.

. . . that bumblebees collect nectar and pollen and produce honey, just like bees?

. . . our largest species of wasp is the hornet? Although it is big and buzzes loudly as it flies it is our most peaceful wasp! It prefers a hole in an old tree, or perhaps an attic to live in.

✦{ MYTH }✦

"Be careful, the bumblebee will burn you!" No, but a sting from a bumblebee is perceived differently than one from a bee or wasp is because it produces a burning sensation. Maybe the myth originated to stop small children from trying to catch cute bumblebees with their hands. In a situation like that they would sting!

"In Asia there are ants that are so strong that they can carry away a child!" The truth is that there is not an ant in the whole world that can carry away a child!

The load that nordic ants can carry to the anthill in their jaws is fairly easy to collect and weigh. According to a study at the Swedish Museum of Natural History, it is mostly dry parts of plants that can weigh between 0.0002 ounces to 0.002 ounces. If you compare the heaviest load with an ant's weight, which is about 0.0004 ounces, the result is that they can carry up to seven times their own weight. But despite their strength ants cannot jump. That is because they can only move their opposite legs at the same time, and never in pairs.

Ants also carry other things to the anthill, like small stones (that weigh up to 0.0015 ounces), dead insects (up to 0.0017 ounces), and rowan berries (at the most 0.0028 ounces). The ants' most common building material, pine needles, weigh about 0.0005 ounces each. Together many ants can carry even heavier loads; for example, a dead hornet, which weighs about 0.0074 ounces.

BLOODSUCKERS AND BATS

Why are some people bitten more often by mosquitoes than others are?

All female mosquitos have to suck blood, in order to obtain enough protein to produce eggs. Why mosquitos sting some people but not others is unknown.

When the female mosquito needs blood, several of her senses are involved, including vision, the sensory system, and smell. Smell is the most important factor when it comes to the female mosquito's search for blood. Depending on wind and humidity, the smell of the human body can reach her from a distance of about 65 feet. Carbon dioxide in the breath, lactic acid in sweat and from the skin, and octenol in sweat, are among the specific substances that attract mosquitoes.

The fact that carbon dioxide from our breath attracts mosquitoes, even at great distances, has been known for a long time. Carbon dioxide also has the ability to increase other smells. For example, mosquitoes are more attracted to the combination of carbon dioxide and lactic acid than only lactic acid or only carbon dioxide. Octenol attracts some mosquitos very strongly while others are repelled and keep their distance. This substance often produces a better reaction when mixed with carbon dioxide.

A SENSE FOR HUMIDITY AND HEAT

The air surrounding a human is a little warmer and more humid. This seems to attract the mosquito. The relative humidity only needs to increase a little in order for the mosquito to feel it. The mosquito is however only attracted to the increased humidity when it is followed by smells or a higher temperature.

Not only humans are affected by mosquitos. Any animal that the mosquito can get near enough to suck blood from will lose a few drops.

THE WORLD'S MOST DANGEROUS ANIMAL?

The small *Anopheles* is probably the world's most dangerous animal. Even if the mosquito in itself is not dangerous, it spreads a parasite that causes malaria, which can be a terminal illness.

Did you know that...

... a mosquito that is full of blood increases its weight from 0.0001 ounces to 0.0003 ounces? That is a weight gain of 333 percent—and it can still fly!

... the Tipuloidea is a big mosquito? But it does not sting!

... that only female mosquitoes suck blood? The males live on the nectar that they drink from flowers.

IF A MOSQUITO IS HIT BY A RAINDROP, WILL IT DIE?

The body of a mosquito is rounded so that its shape will prevent it from hitting the ground because of a raindrop. It also has a very strong outer skeleton that is both jointed and very tough (chitinized), which makes it difficult for a drop to affect the mosquito. In addition, the mosquito has hair, bristles, and a water-repellent layer on its body. All of this makes the possibility of the mosquito being killed by a raindrop very small. Although it could have bad luck of course.

What are ticks good for?

First of all, all animals and plants exist for their own sake! But ticks can also be useful to others by serving as food for birds, spiders, and amphibians.

Ticks are parasitic beings that work as vectors in the ecosystem. That means they transmit bacteria, viruses, and microorganisms from one host to another. Likely they are helpful in regulating the host population by spreading disease, but this is still not very well documented. You can say that ticks have found their own niche in the ecosystem that is not being used by other animals, which makes them successful.

A tick goes through many different stages of development during its life cycle: The first active stage is the larva that can be up to about 0.02 inches. When the larva hatches from the egg, it has six legs and needs a meal of blood before it can develop further. After having sucked itself full of blood from a suitable host, it lets go and falls down to the ground. Here it sheds its skin and moves along to the next stage of development—the nymph. A tick nymph has eight legs and grows up to 0.04 inches long. The nymph also needs a meal of blood before it falls down to the ground, sheds its skin, and moves along to the last active stage—a grown tick with eight legs.

Full-grown male and female ticks mate with each other, but in order for the fertilized eggs to develop inside the female she needs to suck more blood. The male dies after mating without having sucked blood. A female tick can lay up to 1,000 to 3,000 eggs, which are laid one at a time in dense vegetation.

ANESTHESIA!

When a tick bites it first injects an anesthetic substance in its saliva, which prevents the host animal from noticing the bite. How long it is stuck depends on what stage the tick is in. The larvae can suck blood for 3-5 days, while grown females can be stuck from one to two weeks if they are left alone. The tick can use the human as a host in all active stages.

Since ticks are sensitive to dehydration you usually find them near wet areas, often in dense, medium high grass. As a rule they sit at the tip of a grass straw or in low bushes where they can easily catch onto hosts passing by with outstretched front legs. When they have enough blood they let go and simply fall off the blood giver. How fast the tick then needs to find a new host depends on the weather, or rather the humidity, and what stage it is in. The bigger the tick is, the longer it can manage without a new meal of blood.

Ticks have very few natural enemies. They are eaten by birds, spiders, frogs, toads, and lizards—and they are attacked by parasitoid wasps. Our winters rarely cause the ticks any problems. The combination of intense cold and bare ground can be devastating, but usually the weather is mild or a protective layer of snow covers the ground. Two factors that can reduce the number of ticks are if the climate were drier and had fewer hosts, both wild and domesticated. But since both of these things are beyond human control, the possibility to impact the number of tics is very small.

Did you know that...

... most ticks that suck blood from humans, dogs, and cats belong to the species of common tick, *Ixodes ricinus?* There are also other species of ticks that can bite us but about 95 percent of all attacks are made by a common tick.

... the best and easiest way to remove a tick is to as fast as possible pull it off with the help of a special tick remover or tweezers. The quicker you remove it, the less the risk that the tick has any time to transfer infectious substances.

Are bats dangerous?

No, but you should treat them like you treat all other wild animals—with respect. If it is necessary to move a bat you should use gloves. Bats usually bite if you hold or squeeze them as a natural behavior when they feel threatened.

Bats do not attack humans. However, they can become worried and start to fly very close if you approach a colony. When bats hunt prey at night, they sometimes come very close since the heat we send off attracts insects, especially mosquitoes, and we become a walking smorgasbord.

Bats are an important part of biodiversity. They are a successful animal group with many different species and a large geographical spread. At the same time bats are very sensitive to changes in the landscape, which means that the spread of human habitats has caused a decrease in bat populations.

All bats are endangered in Sweden. They are also protected by a European convention—Eurobats—that includes the bats' nesting places and important hunting territories. It is therefore prohibited to kill, harm, or disturb bats.

Bats probably always shared property with us humans. Some species simply prefer to live in houses that give them better protection and in addition are warmer and less windy than tree cavities, outdoor basements, or other natural caves. Our houses can be used both during the winter rest and as a summer home when babies are born. As a rule you can find the bat colony on the south side of the house, since it is the warmest. Normally bats do not harm the house they live in. They cannot gnaw and they do not build nests or destroy the house any other way, but only use the small spaces that are already there.

Usually bats hang in the attic next to a chimney or under the tiles or tin roofs. They will not do any harm there and these spaces are drafty enough to prevent any bad smell. If the bats create big colonies in the central walls of the house it can start to smell because of poor ventilation. It can also be noisy during the summer months when babies are in the colony.

STRANGE SOUNDS AND BED BUGS

The female bat usually gives birth to her baby in the middle of the summer. The baby suckles for three to four weeks until it is ready to fly and can start practicing to hunt insects. During their initial growth stage, the female calls the baby with sounds that humans can hear as well. The animals also move around inside the colony, and a scratching and shuffling sound can occur as they move around. In old houses the bedroom is often situated in the same direction

as the bats prefer, south or southwest. When nothing but a thin bedroom wall separates the rooms there is of course a risk of trouble since bats and humans have different daily rhythms.

Bed bugs can sometimes cause a problem in connection to bats. The best time to exterminate bed bugs is in the middle of June or middle of August, so that all bats will have had the time to leave.

CHOOSE THE RIGHT TIME FOR REMOVAL

It can be very difficult to get rid of bats. The only safe way is to renovate the house so that the bats can no longer find a way in. The tiniest bats need an opening only around half an inch big to get through. Covering vents and other openings with fine mesh nets, such as mosquito nets, can therefore be an alternative method of keeping the bats away. Note that you need to be entirely sure that all bats are out of the house before you start!

Between the first of June and the last of August, you should not do anything at all, since that would disturb the bats while they are giving birth to their babies. If you do it anyway, there is a high probability that you will lock adults and babies inside the house, leading to starvation. Aside from the fact that this method of killing is neither legal nor humane, the dead animals will likely cause serious odor problems.

In Sweden there have been recent findings of antibodies against bat rabies, but not the virus, in individual Daubenton's Bats. That means that the animals have encountered bat rabies during their lifetime and that the immune system has been activated. It is recommended that people who work with bats be vaccinated against rabies, and you should always wear gloves if you touch a bat.

Like other mammals, the bat has a variety of different parasites. Most are specific to bats and do not care at all about humans. If you have bats in the attic or roof tiles, there is no risk whatsoever that the pests will affect humans in the house. If you on the other hand share space, for example if you sleep in a loft directly under the roof tiles, there is some risk.

In Sweden bats live only on insects, and their feces therefore mostly contain parts of insects, such as shells and wings. It is completely harmless. Their feces is also very rich in nitrogen and may advantageously be used to fertilize your flowerbeds.

TO SPOT A BAT

The very best way to experience bats is to be with an expert. At dusk you can also stand outside of a house or cave where you know that bats live. If you are lucky you will spot their dark silhouettes against the still-light night sky as they fly out.

Do vampires exist?

Yes, but not in Transylvania! There are three species of vampire bats; all live in South and Central America. One of these bites a hole in the skin and licks blood from mammals and the other two do the same thing to birds. The species that licks blood from mammals, *Desmodus rotundus*, can cause problems for farmers since it sometimes spreads rabies.

The difference between the vampires' diet and the regular bats that eat mosquitoes is really not that big: mosquitoes brimful with mammal blood are practically on a blood diet!

Did you know that...

. . . bats are big consumers of insects and very efficient mosquito hunters? A scientist in England calculated that a bat can eat up to 7,000 mosquitos during one single night. That is almost twice as many as a swallow!

. . . that bats are an important part of biodiversity? As much as twenty percent of the land-dwelling species in Sweden are bats.

CREATURES WITH EIGHT LEGS

What is the deal with spiders and their poison?

Almost all spiders are toxic predators but only a few are dangerous to humans. Out of the world's 35,000 known spider species, only a couple hundred have a bite that is powerful enough to affect us.

Spiders use poison as fast as possible to make sure that their prey is paralyzed or to kill it, and to start digestion. The poison is usually adapted to the type of prey the spider is catching—although no spider aims for humans as their victims. The roughly 700 spider species in Sweden are normally not dangerous to us humans. But some species can, if they are carelessly handled, be provoked to bite. None of them have enough toxins to cause any serious harm and most of them have too

weak of a bite to cut through our skin. There are however a few large spiders whose bite can be painful and
cause local reactions, likely caused by poison and/or
infection.

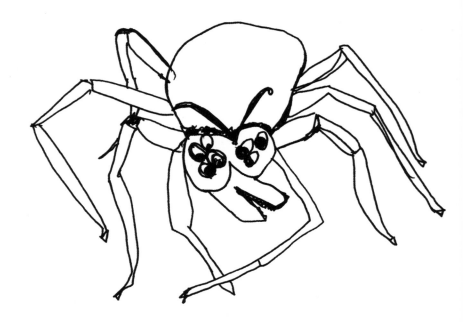

SOME SWEDISH SPIDERS THAT CAN BITE:

> European cave spiders
> Garden spiders and other large species of the orb-weaver family
> Wolf spiders
> Raft spiders
> Common house spiders
> Water spiders
> Yellow sac spiders
> Wasp spiders

There are many theories about which spiders are the most poisonous. Here are some:

> The Australian funnel-web spider *Atrax robustus*, which is often found in damp basements or near swimming pools

> The North American brown spider *Loxosceles recluse*

> The South American banana spider *Phoneutria nigriventer*

> *Latrodectus* spiders, for example the infamous black widow *Latrodectus mactans*

> The Brazilian *Phoneutria fear* is said to have the most toxic venom of all spiders

HEALING DANCE

The tarantula wolf spider, *Tarantula fasciiventris,* gave rise to the tarantella dance. The spider is, despite its size and frightening appearance, only dangerous to the human in especially unfortunate circumstances. Its poison has wrongly been considered to be dangerous to humans and it used to be believed that the only cure for the bitten person was to dance until exhaustion—a tarantella.

Why do spiders spin webs?

Almost all berry pickers have at some point been annoyed with the invisible catching nets that are everywhere in the woods and that get stuck in your face and hair when you walk between two trees.

During almost their entire life, spiders are involved with spinning threads. Aside from producing nets for catching prey, the threads have many other functions. They are used for making nests, passages, constructing the cocoon around the female spider's eggs, camouflaging, and even protecting against the sun. Many spiders trap their prey in threads that make them look like mummies. Before mating, all males weave a special container in which they deposit the sperm that is going to be transferred to the female. Some species' females weave a cocoon around the male after mating. With others, for example crab spiders, the male weaves around the female before they mate.

Most spiders also produce a thread that is used as a safety line. It is secreted when the spider crawls off the web and is regularly attached to the surface with a little dab of glue. Many small spiders and spider babies use the thread for flying, as they can drift off with the wind attached to it, which is a way for the spiders to spread out to new places.

SPIDERS IN THE CEILING

Spiders have claws on their feet. You can see this with a magnifying glass. After that it gets more complicated,

130

because spiders also have thousands of small hairs on their feet. These can only be seen in a very strong microscope. On one spider 78,000 hairs were found on each foot. All of these small hairs make it possible for the spider to walk on the ceiling because the hairs increase the friction against the surface—so the more and smaller hairs the better. Calculations were made considering the spider's weight (0.0005 oz) and under the circumstances that it had all eight legs in the ceiling at the same time with a total of 624,000 small hairs. This gives the spider a safety margin of 160 times, meaning the force that holds it on the ceiling could manage to hold a spider that is 160 times heavier. Flies use a similar method to walk on the ceiling.

A WALKING SILK FACTORY

In the rear body of an orb-weaver spider, there are up to seven different types of glands that produce threads. The most important are *ampullate*, which makes the threads on the edges of the wheel web; *piriform*, which produces silk to keep the separate threads of the web together; *aciniform*, whose threads are used to mummify prey and produce the container for semen and the *tubuliform*, which produces silk for the egg cocoon. This last gland does not exist on male spiders.

Did you know that...

... many spiders move around by using the wind? They climb a tree or another place high up and let out threads that the wind catches on to. That way the spiders can end up anywhere.

... there are spiders that live in water? One of them is the water spider, which weaves a little diving bell that it fills with air in order to breathe under the surface.

... many spider species in Sweden live for one to two years, but some foreign tarantulas can live more than 20 years?

... ticks are arachnids? Scorpions, pseudoscorpions, and acari are also included in the arachnid family.

... arachnids' bodies are split into a front body part and a rear body part. That separates them from insects, whose body is split in three, since the head forms a body part of its own. Arachnids have four sets of legs; insects only have three sets.

HELP
YOUR
NEIGHBORS

SMALL BIRDS

What do birds like to eat?

Feeding small birds during the colder time of the year is both exciting and fascinating. Close up we can study their behavior, appearance, and the differences between sexes; how to separate old birds from young; and many other similarities and differences between the different species.

During a cold winter, a well-stocked bird table can make the difference between life and death for many small birds. So what should you be serving? Depending on the environment and in what part of the country you are, there are different bird species outside your window. Some are generalists and eat practically anything, while others are more specialized and only eat a certain type of food.

Generally the trick is to feed the birds with as much carbohydrates and fat as possible. The birds usually have a good sense of what is appropriate for them. If you feel unsure, you can start by offering a few different types of seeds. You quickly learn what type they eat the most.

If you live near a garden, park, or forest the *sunflower seed* is a perfect option. In city environment or near farmland a *mixture* of different seeds tends to be better than only sunflower seeds. It is always good to complement the seed diet with other food. A wider variety of food where the birds can choose between different things attracts different bird species. Besides seeds you can offer suet balls, bags of nuts, raisins, cubes of cheese, apples, cookies, and sweet bread. In short, there are plenty of things to offer!

Some bird species only eat on the ground, while others like to eat from different types of bird feeders, or peck at suet balls and bags of nuts. Choose different spots to place the food. That lowers the risk of infection, and it is more similar to natural conditions. If you place the bird food in open spaces you are likely to have less visits from birds. It is better to serve it close to a bush, where the birds will feel safer if a sparrow hawk or another predatory bird were to show up, hoping for a feast.

HAVE TO DRINK AS WELL

Birds need to drink water to replace what is lost through feces and exhaled air, and to some extent through the skin. Birds lack sweat glands so no water is lost through sweat.

Snow is frozen water and during the winter the birds to a certain extent obtain fluids through the snow, if there is no access to open water.

Small birds drink by dipping their beak in the water so that the cavities in their mouth are filled by capillary force and surface tension. They can fill their beaks very quickly, but it takes from three to five times as long for the water to flow down the throat through the lifted beak.

SATURDAY SWEETS!

A favorite among many birds is oats. The grains are even more desirable if you drench them in canola oil or some other vegetable oil and let the mixture stand overnight.

THINK ABOUT THE FOLLOWING

To avoid infections it is important to keep good hygiene at the bird table:

> Use bird tables that the birds cannot walk around on to avoid contaminating the food with feces.

> Regularly rake or sweep up leftover food and other waste under the bird table.

> Wash your hands when you have placed food on, or cleaned, the bird table.

> Bird food can attract uninvited guests like voles, mice, and other rodents, which is important to consider—especially in a city environment. If you live in a townhouse you should ask the owner if it is even allowed at all to feed birds.

TOP TEN OF THE BIRD TABLE

1. Great Tit
2. Brambling
3. Tree Sparrow
4. Blue Tit
5. Yellowhammer
6. Blackbird
7. Greenfinch
8. Bullfinch
9. Magpie
10. Bohemian Waxwing

Source: Sweden Ornithological Society's (SOF) inventory "Winter birds near the house 2010". 19 500 persons counted almost 1 150 000 birds.

Did you know that...

... bird houses can be placed south, southwest, or west? If the house is big enough there should not be any problems with overheating.

... the nuthatch likes to live in bird houses but does not settle for just any type of entrance? It has a habit of walling the entrance with dirt, mud, and its own saliva so that the hole exactly fits its body shape. It also walls other cracks and gaps in the house so that no light can get in.

SPEAKING OF

It used to be important to note from what direction you heard the cuckoo sing for the first time in spring. The best would be to hear it sing from the west: If you heard it from the east it meant ease in the coming season, and from the north meant grief. It was the worst to hear it from the south because it foretold that the person hearing it would soon die.

How can you stop birds from flying into windows?

Sometimes you may find small birds that are unconscious or in worst cases dead on the ground under one of your windows. It is especially common if the windows are placed so that you can see right through the house.

Sometimes the bird breaks its neck when it hits the window, but usually it manages to survive. Often it just flies on, although sometimes the bird can become temporarily knocked out and fall down on the ground. It is then in great danger of being caught by a predatory bird. If you find a lifeless bird under the window you should pick it up and put it in, for example, a shoebox with a cover and keep in a protected place inside. After an hour or so, peek inside and see if the bird has come around. Then you can set it free again, outside.

When birds can see a tree or the sky on the other side of a window they think that the coast is clear, and do not notice the window. Therefore you should try to stop them from seeing straight through the house. Drawn curtains can be enough. Another method is to place silhouettes of predatory birds on the windows. The silhouettes are frightening, especially if they resemble a bigger bird gliding in a high altitude ready to attack. Birds never fly towards a predatory bird, only away from it.

It also happens that predatory birds are the direct cause of small birds flying into the window. In the wintertime it is not unusual for hungry sparrowhawks to visit the bird tables. Sparrowhawks have a sneaky way of hunting that lets them suddenly show up in the midst of all the eating birds. When the small birds discover the predatory bird they fly in panic in all directions, and it frequently happens that some of them fly in the direction of a window. It also happens that the hunting predatory bird is so focused on its chase that it flies straight into a window. Predatory birds can then break their necks as well, temporarily pass out, or just fly on as if nothing happened—and then probably without any catch.

BUTTERFLIES

Can you attract butterflies to your garden?

A garden can be made butterfly friendly fairly easily if you plant colorful plants rich in nectar. With the help of these you will get many visits from our most beautiful butterflies. A shallow bird bath attracts both butterflies and birds that can sit and drink on the edge.

The number of butterflies is decreasing, and one of the main reasons is that fields and meadows are overgrown, causing many of the plants that are important to butterflies to disappear. The missing plants were either hosts for larvae or nectar plants for the grown butterflies. By supplementing existing flower beds and bushes with appropriate nectar plants and hosts for larvae, you can help the butterflies. Few but large populations usually have greater attraction ability than many and small populations do.

Especially suitable butterfly plants are Coltsfoot and dandelion in the spring, and other plants from the sunflower family during the rest of the year, like oxeye daisies and different types of asters. Herbs are often perfect for butterflies—and for many wild bees—but they are also not attractive for Roe deer! Flowering bushes like honeysuckle, lilac, and *spiraea* give nutrition to butterflies as well as moths. But few plants can compete with the buddleja in being a butterfly magnet. Therefore it is also known as butterfly bush. It blooms June–August and sometimes in September, and there are several named species with different heights, from about 3.2 feet to 9.8 feet high.

BUTTERFLIES HAVE STICKS

Butterflies are categorized into butterflies and moths. There is no easy and certain way of separating the two groups by looks. A good way however would be to look at the antennae; a butterfly almost always has a thicker part at the end, like a little stick, while moths' antennae often are thin without a stick. Some male moths have feather-like antennae, to sense the female's smell from far away. Another difference is that the butterflies often have colorful patterns and are active during daytime, while moths are mostly camouflaged and active during nighttime. This rule does however have many exceptions. For the most part it is relatively easy to spot butterflies by using good guidebooks.

BEAUTIFUL BUTTERFLIES TO
LOOK FOR IN THE GARDEN

> Small Tortoiseshell
> European Peacock
> Common Brimstone
> Red Admiral
> Painted Lady
> Heliconians
> Polyommatini

With simple measures our golf courses could contribute a great deal to biodiversity without any greater costs. The golf course in itself, *the fairway*, is indeed inevitably a grassy dessert. But meadows could easily be created around it, *the ruff*, with lots of wild flowers. By planting suitable host plants for the butterfly larvae and making sure there is an abundance of plants with nectar for the butterflies during the whole season, you would do butterflies as well as humans a great favor.

NECTAR PLANTS THAT FEEDS FULL-GROWN BUTTERFLIES

> Yarrow
> Asters
> Buddleja
> Borage
> Thistle
> Horse-heal
> Lavender
> Oxeye daisy
> Catnip
> Oregano

Did you know that...

. . . the world's biggest butterfly is the Hercules moth *Coscinocera hercules?* It has a wingspan of about 100 square inches—almost as big as a sheet of paper. The Hercules moth exists in tropical Australia and New Guinea.

. . . Sweden's largest butterfly is the Apollo, whose big females' wingspan can measure up to 4 inches? Also big females of the Poplar Admiral and the Old World Swallowtail have in a few cases reached a wingspan length of almost 4 inches.

. . . Sweden's smallest butterfly is called Polyommatini? It has a wingspan of only 0.7-0.9 inches.

. . . 2,821 butterfly species have been observed in Sweden, but only 120 are butterflies?

. . . 504 of our butterfly species can be found on the IUCN red list of endangered species (as of 2010)? Out of these, 25 species are critically endangered and 73 are endangered.

. . . Thaumetopoeidaes are the only very "dangerous" butterfly larvae that can cause big problems to sensitive people?

150

HOST PLANTS THAT FEED BUTTERFLY LARVAE

> Cabbage, rapeseed — Cabbage butterfly, Small Cabbage White, and Green-veined white

> Thistles — Painted Lady

> Wild strawberries — Grizzled Skipper

> Ribes — Comma

> Blackberries — Green Hairstreak

> Sorrels — Small copper

> Clover — Mazarine Blue

> Stinging nettle — Red Admiral

> Tufted vetch — Polyommatini

> Viola — Heliconians

What does a butterfly larva eat?

The life cycle of a butterfly is fascinating: a crawling, live larva hatches from the egg, to then change into a fairly immobilized cocoon before the full-grown butterfly finally spreads its wings. With a little care and patience it is possible to observe the exciting transformations close up.

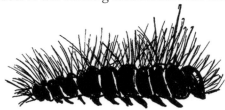

If you want to take a butterfly larva home, you should memorize what plant it was sitting on when you found it. It is a good idea to bring home a leaf or the whole plant, since it probably is the food that the larva likes the most. If you are unsure of what the larva eats you can give it a few different sorts of leaves or plants, picked around the area where you found the larva.

If the larva is not full-grown you can feed it with its host plant in a plastic bag or a glass jar with holes in the lid. When it starts looking a bit dull and stops eating, that usually means it is about to pupate. If it is a butterfly the larva usually pupate above the ground, often sitting on a stick or a straw. Moth larvae pupating dig themselves completely underground; if it's a moth larva, you can fill a jar with mixed soil about 2 inches deep and place the larva there. Then leave it alone for around two weeks.

Whether the larva is a butterfly or a moth, you can place them to hibernate in the refrigerator or outside in a frost free place.

WATCH OUT FOR HAIRY CREATURES!

While we are still at the theme of larvae, a word of caution: Beware of long-haired creatures; you should just let them stay in nature. Many of these larvae have nettle cells in the hairs that will burn our skin when they touch us. The hairs can unfortunately cause allergies or strong itchiness. Because of the hairs most birds avoid eating these larvae. The cuckoo is an exception that somehow manages to eat the hairy larvae.

PUPA TURNS INTO BUTTERFLY

Many butterflies rest over the winter as pupae and normally spend it at a frost free depth in the ground, in some cavity or other protected spot. You could make a hibernating place friendly for your butterfly pupae outdoors, for example on a balcony or the porch. Place a layer of moss and leaves in the bottom of a small glass, plastic jar, or a box, and place the butterfly pupa on top. Then place a layer of moss and leaves on top and preferably also around the jar. It is important that the pupa is protected from sunlight.

Boxes that contain pupae cannot be subjected to frost or too much cold. You can put the jar in a wooden box with a lid that has fairly big drilled holes in the bottom. The wooden box should stand on a couple of wood pieces so that it is a little elevated from the ground, and protected from snow and rain.

You can take the jar inside to room temperature in January at the earliest. If you know what butterfly species it is you can take the jar inside a couple of weeks before its counterparts in nature are ready to fly off. It is important that the pupae are not subjected to a rapid temperature change; a vestibule or a basement can therefore be a suitable stop in between. After that the pupae should be kept as humid as possible but not enough to mold. When the butterflies hatch after a couple of weeks, it is important that they can climb up on a stick, a piece of fabric, or something similar so that the blood quickly reaches the wing ribs; that makes the wings dry as straight as possible. Good luck!

MORE NATURE IN THE GARDEN

Take good care of your garden so that it becomes as varied as possible. A mosaic of flowering herbs, uncut and cut areas of grass, and a few bushes here and there will attract not only beautiful butterflies; birds like it and perhaps a hedgehog will visit you. To watch a hedgehog root around in the dusk is a great adventure! The hedgehog's natural diet consists of snails, worms, insects, and larvae. Amphibians and reptiles are also included in their diet, as well as dead animals. Sometimes it eats vegetables and fallen fruit, although that is more rare.

If you want to create nice food for hedgehogs you can use regular dry dog and cat food. Soak until it turns soft. The hedgehog should not drink milk, as it will get a stomach ache, therefore only give it water.

Did you know that...

... the hedgehog makes many different sounds? It coughs, sputters, sniffles, and snorts. If scared or in pain it gives off a shrill cry.

... a hedgehog has thousands of quills? One of the conservators at the Swedish Museum of Natural History counted the quills on an adult hedgehog and reached the number of 6,000 unbendable, hard quills. Additionally it had about 1,500 bendable, soft quills.

BUMBLEBEES AND BEES

Can you build nests for bumblebees?

Bumblebees are very useful in nature because they pollinate our flowers. Most bumblebee species live underground, usually in abandoned vole or mice passages. You can however build artificial nests for bumblebees above ground.

A nest should have two rooms—one antechamber and a second chamber. The antechamber has an entrance hole that you can close, as well as a device for feeding with sugar solution. You should also be able to place pollen-giving flowers in the antechamber. From the antechamber to the second chamber there should be a passage outfitted with suitable nesting material, for example withered grass or moss.

The whole nest can benefit from being surrounded by extra walls to protect it from light and temperature changes.

Strong heat from the sun, as well as night frost and other strong cold, should be prevented.

NOT HARMFUL

Wild bees that live above ground often build in cavities in trees but usually any type of hole is fine, as long as it is deep enough. A crack in the house wall, an old tube lying around or even a keyhole can be good enough! Bees that nest like this are absolutely not pests. They are only using a cavity that already existed.

UNDERGROUND FRIENDS

About half of our wild bees build nests in existing cavities above ground. The rest dig their own nests in the ground. You can expect a visit from nest-building bees in dirt piles, under the porch, or in another spot that is easy to dig in your garden. The bees are completely harmless unless you provoke them. The best thing to do is to let them keep on with their nesting. If you need to transport, for example, dirt piles away from your garden and wild bees are already nesting there, it is best if you can wait until next spring when the new bees have hatched and flown out. If they are removed before that the larvae and pupae will probably die.

The female lays her fertilized eggs one at a time, usually in a row, and separates them with a thin coat so that a little room, called a cell, is created for each egg. In each egg cell she puts food for the soon to be larvae in the shape of pollen or paralyzed prey, all depending on species. When all of the cavitities are filled, she walls the hole with mud or wax.

When the eggs begin to hatch, the larvae start eating the food and when it is finished they pupate and rest in the cavity over the winter. In the spring the pupae are hatched and the full-grown bees chew their way through the hole and fly out. The bees closest to the exit are hatched first and, therefore, no one gets stuck in the hole. The males are closest to the exist and are thus hatched first, while the females are in the back of the pipe or cavity and hatch last.

Did you know that...

... a bumblebee can carry a load of pollen that weighs over 0.001 oz on their rear legs and a honey bee can carry 0.0004 oz? That is an equivalent of six and sixteen percent of their own weight!

WHAT TO DO IF YOU. . .

. . .find a butterfly larva in the autumn?
One advice is to let the larva dig down in a jar filled with
4-6 inches of loose soil mixed with sand, and on the very top
place a layer of leaves. That way it has the greatest chances of
survival.

. . .find a stag beetle?
The stag beetle belongs in areas with oak trees and is still fairly
spread out in the southeastern parts of the country. Especially
in dawn you could, with a little bit of luck, catch a glimpse of
the giant beetles flying. The larva needs 4-5 years to develop
and lives in decayed wood. Oak stumps are the most common
places, but other stumps of leafy trees or piles of sawdust are
good enough. If you find a lost stag beetle you can let it out in
dawn and hope that it finds its way back for the next day. The
very best thing is to transport it to an area with oak trees.

An employee of the Swedish Museum of Natural History collected and weighed a few different insects. The insects were full-grown, adult individuals. Here are their weights:

Wart-biter	0.06 oz
Humblebee	0.018 oz
Cabbage Butterfly, male	0.007 oz
Honey Bee	0.0028 oz
Wasp, a worker	0.0021 oz
Seven-spotted ladybug	0.0012 oz
Earwig	0.0010 oz
Horse ant	0.0004 oz
Mosquito	0.0001 oz

Did you know that...

... the stag beetle is one of Sweden's heaviest insects? The size of the stag beetle varies a great deal; the largest males can get up to 3 inches long and weigh between 0.14-0.28 oz, but some individuals can be as small as 1 inch. The females also vary in size and can get up to 1.1-1.7 inches long. The stag beetle is the landscape insect of Blekinge.

SOME
SCIENCE

LET'S START FROM THE BEGINNING

What is life?

We all have a fairly good perception of what life *means*. If you were about to try to define the word life, it would be associated with transformation of energy and metabolism, ability to reproduce, ability to perceive surroundings, and development and evolution.

The first life forms on earth were organisms that lived in an ancient sea. Water is an excellent solvent for most substances that an organism needs, and to live in water is comparatively easy. To live on land you have to "bring" water to you in order to not dry out.

The first land-dwelling organisms were probably bacteria, algae, and fungus that lived by the water's edge and at times were exposed to drought. The ones that could best handle the drought could reproduce and their offspring then became better suited to live in a drier environment. Eventually, over millions of years, life made it further and further up on land and more advanced organisms could make the same journey that the microorganisms once had made. Many different ways of handling the precious water were developed. We who live on land carry water inside our bodies!

Plants and animals are structured by cells with a cell nucleus that is surrounded by a membrane. Animals are multicellular organisms that belong to the kingdom *Animalia*. They are mobile and depend on eating other dead or living organisms to stay alive. With few exceptions, animals have muscles, a nervous system, and an inner cavity in the body meant to process food. Unlike plants, the body cells of animals are not surrounded by a shell of cellulose and they cannot utilize carbohydrates through photosynthesis like plants do. Animals are therefore dependent on eating other organisms.

Why did the dinosaurs die?

Throughout the years a variety of theories have been presented about why the dinosaurs went extinct. Today the so called collision theory is considered to be the most probable.

At the start of the 1980s, the most commonly accepted theory today was launched. According to this a giant asteroid or comet collided with the earth 65 million years ago. It had a diameter of at least six miles and the collision probably caused large fires all around the world. The soot from all the fire as well as dust from the explosion would have blocked out all sunlight for several months, maybe even years. Without sunlight the photosynthesis of the plants ended and consequently all ecosystems on land and in the sea collapsed. In addition, the temperature significantly lowered and the cold probably lasted for a long time, which resulted in the animals not already dead from starvation dying anyway. The crash site was presumably the Chicxulub crater situated on the Yucatán Peninsula in Mexico.

Another, not as likely, alternative to the collision theory is that giant volcano ruptures took place on the Indian peninsula. These resulted in a change of the atmospheric composition and the radical decline of the earth's climate. Acid rain also hit the earth, and ozone layers might have been destroyed, which led to a dangerous ultraviolet radiation reaching the surface of the earth.

Here are another few theories as to why the dinosaurs went extinct:

> A hormonal disorder in the dinosaurs made their egg shells too hard or too soft.
> A change in temperature led to only one sex of the dinosaurs being born. We know that the surrounding temperature decides the sex of the fetus in closely related animal groups like sea turtles.
> The levels of oxygen on Earth decreased so that larger animals could not survive.

Many of these theories are relatively poorly founded and have not taken into account that many other groups of animals disappeared at the same time. The fact that a mass extinction occurred made the scientists realize that the conditions for life on Earth must have radically deteriorated at the end of the Cretaceous period around 65 million years ago.

INSECTS VERSUS DINOSAURS

Unlike the dinosaurs, insects have succesfully survived all the way to our time. Of today's known species, 80 percent are insects! Perhaps difference in body size is an important explanation as to why the insects outlived the dinosaurs. There is in fact a connection between an animal's body mass, the "skin," that makes it a little easier for small organisms to adapt when the world around them is changing. Small insects have a bigger body surface area in relation to

171

the body surface area of large dinosaurs. The dinosaurs were likely cold blooded, just like insects, and thus dependent on the sun's heat to be able to move and stay active. The tiny insect heats up quickly thanks to the relatively large body mass area, but for the huge dinosaur it takes longer. It also takes a longer time for the animal to cool down if it gets overheated. Thus big animals are more sensitive to rapid changes in the climate, such as sudden cold or heat. Small insects also have the benefit of being able to seek protection by crawling into the ground—many insects can survive a forest fire that way.

Insects can live in water, on land, and in the air. They can handle hot deserts and freezing temperatures, and can even survive radioactivity. In experiments where insects' reproduction is studied you usually sterilize males with radioactive radiation in dosages that are harmful for human beings. The treatment inactivates the sperm's germ plasm but the mobility of the sperm is not affected. The insect itself does not seem to incur any damage. This has been tried for insect population control: when letting sterile males mate with fertile females, the result is that they have no babies!

How can you know what the dinosaurs looked like?

———

One way of seeing if an animal has been on Earth is to find remains of it. The most common thing is to find fossilized parts of animals or other organisms. Another way is to find animals that have been stuck in resin and, with time, changed into amber.

Fossils from dinosaurs can be seen in museums all around the world. When you find a fossil you always compare it to the ones that are already in the museum's collections or that are illustrated in books. That way you try to reach a conclusion of what you have found. Of course nobody knows exactly what a dinosaur looked like. For example, colors are not preserved in a fossil, but there are prints of what the skin structure looked like. The more fossils are found from a species, the more realistic the reconstruction will be.

Did you know that...

... birds are the dinosaurs of today? The very big dinosaurs died 65 million years ago but some few feathered species lived on. Our birds today are descended from them. The first bird is called *Archeopteryx*.

... a little Blue Tit is more closely related to dinosaurs than big reptiles like crocodiles and turtles are?

... traces of the first cockroaches are about 350 million years old?

... many insects keep their egg in tough capsules that makes it possible for the fertilized egg to survive strong heat and dehydration?

... there have been dinosaurs in Sweden? In Skåne there have been findings of *Plateosaurus*, which was an early, plant eating dinosaur. It walked on all fours but could stand on two feet and ate leaves from tree tops.

Why did the mammoth go extinct?

Most mammoths died at the end of the last ice age. The humans' intensive hunting has up until now been seen as the cause of rapid extinction of larger mammals, but climate change caused by humans has also been discussed. Recently mammoth DNA has been found in Alaska, which shows that the animals existed at least 2,600 years longer than what was previously thought. That means that mammoths and humans have lived side by side. For this reason the hypothesis of human hunting can be written off, and only climate change remains.

There are about 25 findings of mammoth bones in Sweden. The findings have been made from Skåne in the south to Jämtland in the north. The finding spots can in general be divided into three groups: one in southern Sweden, one in western Sweden, and one in central Sweden. The oldest finding was fragments from a tusk that was found outside of Svedala in Skåne 1865 or 1866. The latest finding was made in Kånkback in Jämtland 1975. The southern and western Swedish findings are between 22,000 and 32,000 years old, which means that they lived in Scandinavia during an interstadial (a warm period during an ice age). The central Swedish mammoths are dated to another interstadial—the Jämtland interstadial—which occurred 45,000–55,000 years ago. We cannot be sure of the age of the "Stockholm mammoth," but it probably lived during the Jämtland interstadial as well.

"We need to know when the domesticated cat and the fox came to Sweden and Östergötland. Did the fox exist here during the Viking age? Supposedly there are many species of fox."

- -

It is not easy to answer that question. What we know with certainty is that the domesticated cat existed in southern Sweden during the Stone Age. As for foxes we know that they existed during the late glacial time (17,000-11,500 years ago). But it is uncertain if there were red or arctic foxes.

A LITTLE SOMETHING ABOUT SPECIES AND NAMES

How do you define a species?

It used to be that two individuals were considered to belong to the same species if they could reproduce and have fertile offspring. Today there are several concepts of species.

When we started classifying animals and plants and separating them into different species, appearance and body structure were important. Individuals with common external charcteristics were considered to be one species, and individuals that looked different would be considered a different species. This is usually referred to as the *morphological species concept*. It was created by Carl von Linné and used a bit into the 1900s. Morphology means appearance.

During the 1940s the *biological species concept* was introduced, which can be expressed as two individuals belonging to the same species if they can have babies together, which in their turn can have babies. It also means that if two individuals (that are completely healthy and of different sexes) cannot have babies together they belong to different species. A golden retriever and a bulldog look completely different but can very well have babies together, which eventually can become parents themselves. Despite differences in appearance the golden retriever and bulldog belong to the same species—dog (*Canis domesticus*). A horse and a donkey can have babies together but they will be sterile. Horse (*Equus equus*) and donkey (*Equus asinus*) are in fact two different species, which means that a mutual foal cannot have babies.

However the biological concept of species does not work in all contexts, such as when it comes to organisms where the offspring is produced through asexual reproduction, division, vegetative reproduction, or *parthenogenesis* (no fertilization).

DNA SHOWS THE WAY

In the 1960s the *phylogenetic concept of species* was introduced. Basically, it means that you group animals and plants by trying to reconstruct their relatedness using DNA.

There is no definition of "species" that describes all organisms. There are always a few exceptions for animals that do not function like all other species. Therefore there is a constant lively discussion about the concept of species amongst scientists within biological fields.

If you are unsure of whether or not a newfound little insect belongs to a certain species, you can compare it to the so called specimen. That is the individual that was used to originally describe the species in question, and that is the guide to what that particular species look like. Many specimen are kept at the Museum of Natural History in Stockholm. We compare other individuals with the specimen to see if it is the same species or not. If not, it might be a new species that has to be scientifically described.

NUMBER OF ANIMAL SPECIES IN THE WORLD:

No one can answer exactly how many animal species there are in the entire world, but here is an estimate:

> Mammals   4,800
> Birds   10,000
> Reptiles   8,000
> Amphibians   5,000
> Fish   30,100
> Insects   1,100,000
> Molluscs   70,000
> Arthropods   40,000
> Other animals   130,000

Today there are about 1.5 million known and scientifically described animal species in the world. The insects are by far the largest animal group on earth and the number of species is constantly increasing. Every year about 10,000 new ones are added. As of the year 2002, the number of identified species of insects was estimated to be between one and two million. However there is still no method of compiling information from all the world's collections in one complete directory. That means that nobody has absolute knowledge over how many species of insects have been described at the time of writing.

HOW LONG HAVE THERE BEEN. . .

. . . *lynx?*
The oldest fossil findings of cats are from Miocene, in other words about 25 million years old. About 15 million years ago, the cat's line of development diversified and along one of these branches the lynx originated.

. . . *polar bears?*
The oldest fossils are about 70,000 years old.

. . . *octopuses?*
The oldest fossils of octopuses are about 500 million years old. They belong to a now extinct group of octopuses that are known as *ortoceratiter.* They lived inside straight, tube-shaped shells. Fossils of the shells can today be seen in stairs and window sills made of limestone.

Why is it called a ladybug?

All the way into the 1700s, Latin was the general written language in Sweden, and names of plants, birds, and animals in Swedish were not "needed." Some names have, however, been found to be used a long time ago, but those are mostly names of species that humans were either benefiting from or had trouble with. The first names of insects in Swedish did not show up until the middle of the 1800s, and those were names of pests that would harm forest, fields, or gardens.

A scripture about Scandinavian butterflies published in the year 1853 by the priest Hans Daniel Johan Wallgren is an interesting exception. Here the brimstone is called "Citrongula Tostefjärilen," and is likely to be one of the very first published Swedish names for a species. Toste is an old name for Alder Buckthorn; the brimstones' larvae lives on the leaves of buckthorn, but also on the leaves of the closely related Common Buckthorn.

Even today there are many insect species that lack Swedish names and only have scientific names. These used to be in Latin but can also be Latinized Greek. A scientific name usually consists of two parts—one family name and one species name—and is written in italic. The species name usually describes a character of the species in question but can also be made up from the founder's name.

The way of naming and categorizing most animals comes from 1758 and the tenth edition of Carl von Linné's work *Systema nature*. The classifying system was not only for animals but for all living organisms. According to this system plants and animals are grouped together in a number of systematic categories: The most important categories are (with the brimstone as an example):

Regnum	kingdom	animal	Animalia
Phylum	division	invertebrate animal	Arthropododa
Classis	class	insects	Insecta
Ordo	order	butterflies	Lepidoptera
Familia	family	Pieridae	Pieridae
Genus	genus	brimstones	*Gonepteryx*
Species	species	brimstones	*Gonepteryx rhamni*

189

. . . *vertebrates* are animals with backbones that also used to be called Craniatas or Craniotas?

. . . *invertebrates* are animals without backbones?

. . . the butterfly's scientific name *Lepidoptera* comes from Greek and means "scaly wings"?

. . . the Praying Mantis was named from the way it holds its front legs together, just like when we pray?

SMOKY FLIES

The term "smoke flies" refers to flies that swarm in smoke from fires. In Sweden it occurs among the species *Microsania pectipennis* and *Hormopeza obliterata*. The latter is very unusual and is found on the national red list of endangered species.

Smoke flies do not really exist as a group of their own amongst insects, and neither is it a technically accepted name.

Atlantic herring or baltic herring

Baltic herring is a Baltic Sea variant of the species herring, more specifically the herring that can be found north of Kalmar. It is not unusual that the same species has a different name depending on where it was found or how it behaves in the country.

This means that Baltic herring and Atlantic herring are the same species. They do differ a little. Baltic herrings are usually not more than 6-8 inches long and have relatively long heads, while Atlantic herrings are 10-15 inches long and have shorter heads. The Atlantic herring has had many Swedish names. Most can be related to where they have been found, for example bank herring, reef herring, coast herring, bay herring, archipelago herring, hill herring, grass herring, Blekinge herring, Gotland herring, Mörkös herring, sea herring, or fjord herring. Size has also affected names, for example large herring, small herring, full herring, or food herring. The seasons have also affected the names: spring herring, autumn herring, winter herring, and ice herring.

"Atlantic Herring and Baltic Herring are of the same species and only differ in size."

Carl von Linné 1751

Common Swift or Barn Swallow?

The Common Swift was known as the Barn Swallow far into the second half of the 1900s. It is not strange since the bird resembles a swallow. Systematically, though, it belongs to the family of swifts and should be called Common Swift. The name has taken a long time to reach the public, and you can still hear the names Barn Swallow and Common Swift almost as often. The latter is definitely preferred.

In much the same way, the snow magpie's name was changed to fieldfare in the middle of the 1900s. The fieldfare is a thrush and not a magpie or crow. On the other hand we still have "false" name endings on, for example, the Eurasian Oystercatcher,[1] which is a wader bird and not a crow bird. The name surely originated from the similar feather coating of the black and white magpie.

GAME FISH

Salmon, trout, char, grayling, and other salmon species are often considered to be especially attractive from a game fisherman's point of view and were earlier known as *game fish*. In the plant kingdom the expression is used in the same way for trees whose wood is particularly appreciated and used in fine carpentry.[2]

---

[1] *The Swedish name for the Eurasian Oystercatcher is Shore magpie.*
[2] *The expression for game fish in Swedish is pure fish. The same expression is used for wood: pure wood.*

In the world of birds, you can find the Hoopoe and the Great Grey Shrike. The Hoopoe was considered to foretell war and trouble when troops were approaching, and that is probably from where its name derives[3]. The Great Grey Shrike was earlier known as the watcher or Red-Backed Shrike. When the bird warns it gives off a peculiar shriek. This attribute was earlier used by falconers who kept them to warn about predatory birds.

DIALECTAL NAMES

"Körkmack" is the most common name for the Black-and-Red-bug on Gotland. It is red and black with a little white spot and resembles a beetle to the untrained eye. It occurs from Skåne to Västmanland but is most common in calcareous soil, like on Gotland and Öland. The Black-and-Red-bug is the landscape insect of Gotland.

---

[3] *The Swedish name for the bird is translated as Here bird. The word "here" can also be found in the Swedish word for army, hence the connection of names.*

"Gorm" or "görmsticka" was used in the Västerbotten dialect for botflies, the family *Oestridae*. They are big and soft haired flies whose larvae live as parasites inside the body of bigger mammals. In Sweden three species occur: the ox warble fly, reindeer warble fly, and the sheep nasal botfly. The ox warble fly and the reindeer fly lay eggs on the legs of animals in late summer. When the animals lick their legs the newly hatched larvae make their way into the throat after which they dig into the tissues. Then they wander around the body of the host for half a year, especially in connective tissue and muscles. By the end of the winter they are beneath the skin on the back of the animal and look like bumps where the larvae later come out. The botflies' attack can severely weaken the host animal, and even if the holes after the bumps are healed, the scars reduces the value of the skin.

Did you know that...

. . . the fish that today is known only as trout used to be called salmon trout? The scientific name is *Salmo trutta*. The trout is divided in three subfamilies:

> *Salmo trutta trutta* – Sea trout
> *Salmo trutta lacustris* – Brown trout
> *Salmo trutta fario* – Brown trout

Which are the earliest known birds in Sweden?

Knowledge of birds has with time become better, and the quality of bird books has improved considerably. This has lead to the number of spotted bird species in the country to constantly increase. Some species have however disappeared as hatching birds in Sweden, while others are added.

The earliest known bird in Sweden by far is the raven. It is mentioned on a rune as early as the 500s, the so called Järnbergsstenen in Värmland. The next known species is the Black Grouse, which is documented in Snorre Sturlasson's *Heimskringla*, from the year 1018. The following year, 1019, the crane was mentioned. After that we have to wait almost two hundred years for the nightingale to show up in an inscription in Gamla Lödöse in Västergötland on a rune from around year 1250. In the year 1263 there are reports of the Skylark, without further data of where it was found. It is then not until the 1300s when cuckoo, Northern Lapwing, Eurasian Eagle-Owl, European Nightjar, Rook, Crow (*cornix*), Common Buzzard, and Magpie are mentioned. In the 1400s the Hazel Grouse, Grey Heron, Western Jackdaw, and Western Capercaillie were mentioned as well. In the 1500s, Common Swift, European Goldfinch, Black Woodpecker, European Robin, Common Blackbird, Common Starling, White Wagtail, Chaffinch, and European Greenfinch were added to the list. By the end of the 1600s, 163 bird species had been spotted in Sweden. Not until the 1900s did bird watching really take off and today the list of Swedish birds has 492 species.

The number of bird species that regularly hatch in today's Sweden is 243. That is relatively numerous, which can be explained by the variety of biotopes—habitats—that exist in the country. Sweden is a large and elongated country with coastlines of saline and brackish water. There are lots of large as well as smaller fresh water lakes and rivers. The landscape is hilly and has mountains over 6,560 feet high. Between the coasts and mountains there are forests and fields as well, which have in various ways been affected by humans.

Did you know that...

... birds can be found on all continents on earth?

... there are about 10,000 described bird species in the world?

... a total of 492 bird species have been seen in Sweden as of the year 2009?

... Sweden's most common birds are the Willow Warbler (20-30 million individuals) and Chaffinch (16-30 million individuals)?

198

SPECIES BROUGHT IN BY HUMANS

An unknown species is a species that has been spread outside of its natural range by humans. It can happen on purpose or by mistake.

In recent years the term *invasive* unknown species has become more and more common. *Unknown* and *invasive* are luckily not synonyms. An unknown species is considered to be invasive if its introduction and/or spread threatens the biodiversity, causes socioeconomic damage, or threatens humans' health. Out of the unknown species about ten percent are invasive, invading, and are taking over habitats where they have no natural enemies.

Spanish slug, giant hogweed, and Chinese mitten crab are examples of invasive unknown spices that during the years have made their way into Sweden. They have caused damage in water, on land, and among humans and animals.

A FEW EXAMPLES OF UNKNOWN INVASIVE SPECIES IN SWEDEN

> Spanish slug, came in 1975
> Chinese mitten crab, found for the first time in the 1930s.
> Eurasian Collared Dove came flying in the 1950s or 1960s.
> Muskrat, sneaked into the country in the 1940s or 1950s.
> Raccoon dog, first confirmed finding made in Sweden in 1947.
> Wasp spider, came in the end of the 1990s.
> Round goby, first known finding in July of 2008 in Karlskrona.
> Pacific oyster, discovered in the summer of 2007 on the west coast.
> Warty comb jelly, first found in October 2006 in north of Bohuslän.

When the ice melted during the latest (but not last) ice age, humans started wandering in from the south. But we were not the only ones.

The mammoth immigrated 14,000 years ago, to "quickly" disappear during the same millennium. The polar bear came around 13,000 years ago and managed to stay for nearly 2,000 years before it suffered the same fate.

But more successful were the moose, reindeer, wolf, brown bear, wolverine, and mountain hare. These came about 12,000 years ago, and as we know have settled here.

Of course not only large animals immigrated at this time, but they are the only ones to have left traces today. Many other animals were likely to have immigrated at the same time. For example:

› Fleas and lice
› Crane flies and mosquitos
› Ravens and skylarks
› Salmon and trout
› Lemming and Arctic Fox

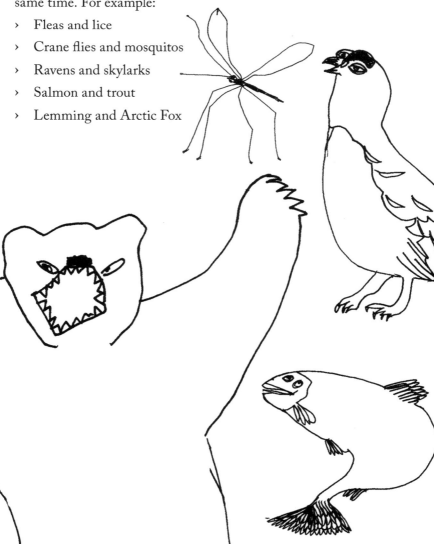

Did you know that...

... nature is just waiting for you to visit? So fill your backpack—don't forget binoculars and a magnifying glass—and get out there!

If you are wondering about something in nature, you can always contact the On Duty Biologist:

e-mail: jourhavande.biolog@nrm.se

www.nrm.se